The Lazy Woman's™ Guide to Just About Everything

Practical Tips & Lazy Wisdom for a Life of Ease

by Judie O'Neill & Bridget Fonger

Terri,

Here's to a lazy life full of love + great friends like Cathi!

♡, Bridget

ELE
PHANT
EYE
prEss

The Lazy Woman's™ Guide to Just About Everything
Practical Tips & Lazy Wisdom for a Life of Ease
is part of the Lazy Woman's series.

The Lazy Woman's™ is a trademark of Judie O'Neill and Bridget Fonger

The authors did an exhaustive (we were tired) search to determine if previously published material included in this book required permission to reprint. We are grateful to all the writers we have quoted for their wisdom and apologize if there are any errors. Please let us know so we may correct them in future editions.

Anything passing as wisdom or advice, lazy or otherwise, contained herein should be taken with a grain of salt and used at your own risk. In other words, the authors and publisher disclaim any liability in connection with the use of this material.

Publisher's Cataloging-in-Publication
(Provided by *Quality Books, Inc.*)

ISBN 0-9711673-0-3

O'Neill, Judie.
    The lazy woman's guide to just about everything :
practical tips & lazy wisdom for a life of ease / Judie
O'Neill & Bridget Fonger. – 1 st ed.
    p.cm.
    Includes biobliographical references and index.
    ISBN: 0-9711673-0-3

    1. Home economics. 2. Self-actualization
(Psychology)   I. Fonger, Bridget. II. Title.

TX145.054 2001   640
                    QB101-201013

Cover and interior illustrations by Bridget Fonger
Book design by Susan Landesmann
Editing by Frances Fusco

Printed in the United States on acid-free paper

This book may be ordered from the publisher,
but please try your local bookstore first!

ELEPHANT EYE PRESS, P.O. Box 50250
Pasadena, CA 91115-0250, Phone: (626) 794-0726

Contact Elephant Eye Press at www.elephanteyepress.com for information about future publications and Lazy Woman events. Of course, we can't stop you from contacting Bridget and Judie directly at lazywoman.com for information about lectures, workshops, future Lazy Woman books and/or for sordid details about the authors' personal lives.

DEDICATION

To our moms for allowing us
to cultivate our Lazy Ways.

To our dads for making us feel
as though we could do anything.

TABLE OF CONTENTS

TABLE OF CONTENTS

"At *heart I am lazy, yet I find such peace
and delight in it that I believe it is a
natural state, and in what looks like my
laziest periods I am closest to my center.*"

– Andre Dubus
A *Father's Story* from *God:Stories*
edited by C. Michael Curtis

THE BIRTH OF A LAZY NOTION
(OR HOW THIS BOOK WAS BORN)

We're happy you've found your way to our book. We "found" it ourselves in a very lazy fashion. At 3:00 a.m. one morning, Judie woke up to these words: The Lazy Woman's Guide to Just About Everything. She knew it would be a book, and saw it as a kind of almanac full of tips and reminders to help women get through the day with a little more ease. A few days later she told the title to Bridget, who had been working on a book about entertaining without stress. Was this meant to be one book? The title alone seemed to personify the vision of what we wanted to create. Our experience of writing the book was like a contemplation, an investigation of what it meant to live the Lazy Woman's Way. It was the title that guided us.

We had worked together many times before, producing fundraisers, events, and parties. In our business, EarthAngels, we hauled away people's junk, recycled the *trash* and refurbished the *treasures*. It was in our workspace that we came up with the philosophy "If it isn't within reach, you don't need it!" which became part of the Lazy Woman's Way. People continued asking our advice about furniture, decorating, and entertaining so the evolution toward hosting Lazy Woman Workshops and writing this book was a natural one.

While the book is filled with lazyquick tips, it is cultivating a lazy inner attitude that is the cornerstone of the Lazy Woman's Way. Early on Bridget dubbed Judie the "The True Lazy Woman." She has been married 36 years, has three lovely grown daughters, is raising a pre-teen son, has been a foster parent to many, worked as a professional designer, and perhaps most importantly has offered her shoulder and ear to many women who have greatly benefited from her wisdom on parenting, marriage, homemaking, designing, gardening, and much more. Judie has a Masters degree in Human Development, has been an elementary school teacher, a parent education teacher, and has consistently worked within her local public school system as an advocate for reform. Currently she is helping cultivate the Odyssey Charter School, where her daughter, Lauren, teaches and her son, Max, attends 7th grade.

As a "Lazy Woman-in-Training," Bridget is working on cultivating the lazier inner attitude of her co-author. She has been a theatre and event producer, marketing & publicity consultant, fundraiser for the non-profit sector and party giver par excellence. As owner of The Angel Store and as a producer, Bridget was forced to come up with many shortcuts to the most beautiful creations. Single for the moment, she lives with her dog, Charlie and cat, Bliss.

There's no way to stop everything that's 'happening' in your life to search for inner peace but in the midst of the madness we both try to create quiet moments and find some serenity within. We invite you to join us on the Lazy Woman's Way. It's definitely a road worth traveling.

Getting Started The Lazy Woman's Way

I magine moving through the day with a sense of ease – even when surrounded by chaos. What if you often felt a sense of calm appreciation most of the time, no matter what was happening around you? We call that the Lazy Woman's Way.

Life is fast-paced and demanding. Women are frazzled and overworked. We are expected to be perfect homemakers, savvy and conscious mothers, sexy partners, spiritually enlightened *and* bring home at least some of the bacon. All of us seek relief from these awesome demands.

We tend to lose ourselves in the working, wifing, mothering, daughtering, and creating. We challenge the myth that bigger, more, harder, and higher mean better. All around us, we see people who work harder, have a bigger house, earn a higher paycheck, and yet they are not happier.

The universe seems to be inspiring a feast of books and tapes that address our desire to "have it all," while simultaneously achieving inner peace, i.e. *How to Achieve Nirvana While Talking on the Cellphone and Jogging on the Treadmill with a Baby on Your Hip*. Writers are crafting beautiful road maps for life-changing journeys — sometimes we even have time to read them. If you're short on time, one avenue to solace may lie in this word: LAZY.

The dictionary and thesaurus define lazy as slothful, allergic to work, idle, loafing, and sluggish. But, we look at lazy a little differently.

Being able to live in a less hurried and less harried way brings rich rewards. We all could use more Hammock Time. It doesn't matter if you're in a Hammock, a hot bath, the garden – or even, for some, the kitchen! The Lazy Woman's Guide to Just About Everything offers the "CliffsNotes" approach to finding the calm within the storm and getting more Hammock Time.

Don't worry: we aren't saying that people should just lie around all day. We aren't saying "DO NOTHING." Nor are we saying "DO EVERYTHING." The difference lies in the choosing. Every day you make decisions - big and small - that shape your life. The trick is being aware of these choices and their effects.

You can choose to live in a way that has less judgment, less concern for appearances, less conflict, and shorter "to do" lists. You can accomplish tasks more simply, leaving you more time and energy for things that truly bring you pleasure. This will create both inner and outer peace. In other words, the Lazy Woman doesn't tend to get her "panties in a bunch."

When you feel overwhelmed and exhausted, you need quick, nurturing alternatives to help calm your nerves, un-push your buttons, or get dinner on the table in ten minutes! With lazyquick tips, check lists, and other short-cut reminders, the Guide's format is quick and easy. It puts the relief you need at your fingertips, whether it's new information or just a reminder of what you already know. You can pick it up for a lazyquick tip or linger with something to soothe your soul. It wouldn't be lazy if it wasn't a sweet and easy read. The Lazy Woman doesn't need to leap or run to happiness. She can meander or stroll there.

And, for those of you who like to know how the story ends before you begin, we welcome you to check out the Lazy Woman's Seven Commandments and the Lazy Woman's Top Ten Practical Tips on the blue pages at the back of the book. In a nutshell, they embody the Lazy Woman's Way.

RELAX...

AND

ENJOY!

Lazy Woman Recliner

A Hammock in Every Room

MAKING A HOME THE LAZY WAY

COOKING

BREAKFAST, LUNCH & DINNER

DINNER PARTIES

HOME DECOR

PAINT

GARDEN

COMPOST

LAUNDRY

CLEANING

INTRODUCTION

We are all weavers. Everything we are or do is part of the thread we use to create the fabrics of our lives — whether we are working to solve an internal issue or are creating something in our exterior lives — it's all part of the tapestry. We can't separate the *being* from the *doing*. What we do is wholly interwoven with what we *feel* and who we *are*.

How we create our homes and how we feel about them impacts us every day. We want to create a rich tapestry, one that is pleasing to our eye and is considered worthy by others, but this can become a source of stress. We forget to enjoy the weaving because we're so focused on the pattern of the cloth, so attached to the fruits of our labor.

Sometimes, what comes off our loom is a fine silk, other times a rough but cherished wool blanket. Then there are the times when we look down at what we've created with disgust and ask "How could I have gone so far astray from my vision?!" It's not always easy to appreciate the piece of cloth that has mistakes or flaws, but the Lazy Woman learns to see that every texture or color has value.

What happens in your home, what comes out of it, the celebrations and losses, the moves, the renewals and remodels, are all part of what makes the tapestry rich. Forgive, accept, and celebrate your creations. Your taste will change, fads will ebb and flow, but the experiences are what everyone will remember.

COOKING

One person's pleasure is another's drudgery. What for some is a passion for creating in the kitchen is for others a life sentence of servitude. If you just love everything about cooking – including the planning, buying, washing, chopping, sautéing and cleaning up – then you are lucky.

> *"You don't get over having to cook, any more than you get over having big feet."*

– Peg Bracken

If you are responsible for three meals a day for anyone other than just yourself, even the most enthusiastic of chefs can long for a break. Fortunately, we live in a time where we have easy access to convenience foods – pre-chopped, pre-washed, pre-cooked – which can lighten the load. Even if you don't use them every day, grabbing a salad-in-a-bag and a frozen pizza on the way home from work can make for a more enjoyable family dinner. (See Breakfast, Lunch & Dinner.)

You can have different standards for cooking on different occasions. A gorgeous, gourmet, nutritionally balanced dinner isn't necessary every night. Even if you love cooking, holding yourself to this high standard all the time is exhausting. Give yourself a break!

LAZYQUICK TIPS
The Lazy Chef

SAUTÉING VEGETABLES

Sauté veggies in a couple tablespoons of water with garlic and olive oil, put a lid on and let the veggies steam for a minute or two. You will cut down your cooking time, use less olive oil, and still have that sautéed flavor.

STEAMING

Steaming is the quickest and healthiest way to cook vegetables. Instead of sautéing, steam them and then add the olive oil with seasonings after cooking.

MICROWAVE PRE-COOK

If you've forgotten to start a long-cooking food or if it's too hot to have the stove/oven on very long, you can partially cook foods in the microwave and transfer them to the stove top or oven to complete the cooking.

• PASTA SAUCE: Put it in the microwave for a few minutes before putting it on the stove (on low heat) to get the flavor percolating.

• BAKED POTATOES/YAMS: Pop them in the microwave for about 5 minutes and they'll take half the time they usually take in the oven.

• BARBECUE: You can pre-cook chicken and throw the partially-cooked meat on the grill and still get that barbecued flavor.

LAZYQUICK TIPS
Lazy Kitchen Helpers

Lazy Women love technology when it's quick and easy. These are some of our favorite kitchen tools (besides the microwave, of course):

PRESSURE COOKER: New electric models turn off automatically and make meals in minutes. Lentils, split peas, beans, rice, soups, and stews can be done in less than half their usual cooking time.

RICE COOKER: Throw in the rice, the water, and turn it on. No monitoring, no burning! Perfect rice every time.

CROCK POT: The best thing about crock pots is that you can take a few minutes in the morning, throw the ingredients in, and know you'll have dinner waiting at the end of a long day.

BREAD MAKER: You literally put the ingredients in the machine and turn it on. It turns itself off when it's done. The smell is divine and it takes about 3 minutes to gather the ingredients!

ELECTRIC ICE CREAM MAKER: Some recipes take almost NO preparation, like fruit ices, others require very little time. Huge culinary bang for your cooking buck!

TOASTER OVEN: Perfect for garlic bread, mini pizzas, and toasting nuts, especially in the summer when you are trying to keep your house cool.

Some of the tips in Dinner Parties and Breakfast, Lunch & Dinner are also good for everyday cooking. No matter which method you choose to make meal preparation easier, just remember that each meal doesn't have to satisfy every gastronomic and nutritional requirement for your family. Sometimes, you want to create a masterpiece and can achieve this. Other times, you just need to make grilled cheese sandwiches. If you do, you might have the time and desire to chat with your husband over a cup of tea or read your child an extra bedtime story.

BREAKFAST, LUNCH & DINNER

Let's say you are preparing dinner and you realize you don't have the last two ingredients. Give it up! Sometimes you have to let go of the idea of what dinner was going to be. Then, open the freezer, the fridge, the cupboard... and improvise! For instance, have breakfast for dinner – make eggs & bacon, pancakes, or French toast. Turn your view of what is appropriate to eat upside down, if that is what it takes to get dinner on the table. Let your kids warm up pizza or leftover spaghetti for breakfast if you are out of milk for your cereal.

Nobody is going to become vitamin-deficient from a few inventive meals.

LAZYQUICK TIPS
How to Make a Meal Out of Anything

• Put a layer of cheese on leftover anything, instant rice, or scrambled eggs; pop it in the toaster oven and you end up with a casserole-like dish.

• Cut up just about anything and scramble it with eggs.

• Put tuna salad on bread, top with sliced tomato, sliced pickles and a little cheese. Put it under the broiler and voilà: *Tuna Lorenzo* (or whatever fancy name you want to give it).

• Potatoes – Bake a potato (or microwave it, if in a hurry), cut it open, butter, salt and pepper it. Then add veggies, chopped chicken/turkey, cheese, sour cream, or whatever you have in the fridge.

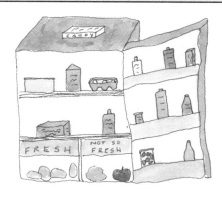

DINNER PARTIES

Lazy Women can have dinner parties too! Whether it's for unexpected guests or a planned event, it doesn't have to be a big production. It can be done quickly and at the last minute. Keeping certain things on hand (in your cupboard or fridge) can make this possible.

The key to making a regular ol' dinner into a party is PRESENTATION! We eat with our eyes first!

It is a well-known fact in the food service industry that you can create a beautiful culinary experience by taking average food and displaying it wonderfully. A party is about gathering a little bit of beauty, good food, and nice people!

LAZYQUICK TIPS
Party Staples to Have on Hand

You can create a dinner party in less than an hour if you have a couple of the right things in your freezer, fridge and/or cupboard. Try out different brands on your family, then stock the ones that make the cut.

FREEZER

Some frozen food doesn't look or taste frozen once it has been cooked and garnished. Try to keep fresh herbs on hand (parsley and basil are our favorites because you almost can't misuse them). Chop a little bit up and sprinkle it over the top after you have heated your frozen entrée, then bunch up a few sprigs and put them around the dish with maybe a few sliced tomatoes, and you have something that looks and smells homemade. We always keep our favorite frozen lasagna in the freezer. It's beautiful, easy, and impressive when served with a salad.

There are also some great frozen hors d'oeuvres and desserts on the market. Try some out and stock your favorites. Garnish an hors d'oeuvre plate with fresh herbs and serve thaw-and-serve cake topped and circled with fresh flowers.

continued...

FREEZER STAPLES THAT WE LIKE: lasagna, edamame, mini-quiches, peas, corn, broccoli florets, sausage, frozen sourdough rolls, gourmet cheesecakes and tortes.

CUPBOARD

Some canned and boxed foods can be very tasty and look special enough to serve for company. For a quick and casual get-together: a favorite packaged soup can be served in a beautiful bowl with a touch of chopped herbs, grated cheese, or a drizzle of cream on top. Serve with a basket of bread or crackers and a salad.

CUPBOARD STAPLES THAT WE LIKE: olives, olive oil, capers, Ortega diced green chilies, canned crab, Knorr leek soup mix & onion soup mix, instant seasoned rices, pasta sauces, pizza sauce, good crackers, tortilla chips.

REFRIGERATOR

Figure out what your family eats regularly and make your last minute dinner party menus according to those fresh items. Here are some of the things we keep in our refrigerators:

LETTUCE: Fresh bagged mixed lettuce is pre-washed and salad ready.

continued...

CHEESE: Gourmet cheeses like goat, feta, and gorgonzola can be used on salads, pasta, and vegetables. Shredded cheeses are great as a topping for soups and casseroles.

BUTTER & OLIVE OIL/CREAM/MILK: Anything sautéed in a little butter and/or olive oil is instantly tasty. Cream (half-and-half or whole milk) is a great enhancer to sauces and soups. Toss a splash of cream and a little butter on steamed cabbage.

LEMONS: Lemon and olive oil is our favorite dressing for salads, vegetables, fish, and chicken. Squeeze lemon juice over the food and then drizzle on a little olive oil; add salt and pepper to taste. You almost can't mess it up, but err on the side of being too light. Keep tasting it until you have the right balance.

TOASTED NUTS: It's good to have a pre-toasted supply of nuts to add homemade accents to your frozen or pre-made foods. Our favorites: toasted pine nuts (sprinkled over any Italian dishes and/or on your accompanying salad or side dish); toasted pecans or walnuts (chopped up in instant rices and/or sprinkled over salads with a little gorgonzola cheese).

REFRIGERATOR STAPLES THAT WE LIKE: lemons, bagged (pre-washed) mixed salad, pre-shredded and gourmet cheeses, pepperoni/salami, butter, half-and-half (or milk), potatoes, fresh herbs (see Garden).

LAZYQUICK TIPS
Party Accents

A beautifully set table doesn't take much effort but help sets the tone for your party. Again, major bang for your time buck.

COLOR: Color is your unifying element. Pick a color (or two) from your china and linen. Then when you throw together a last minute dinner party, your table design will be easier.

TABLE COVERING: Tablecloths, large pieces of fabric/lace/brocade/tulle, runners, table toppers (buy them at sales, linen outlets, etc.) can be combined and layered according to your party motif.

FLOWERS: If you don't have a garden, grab a bouquet at the market. If you have shrubbery, make a bouquet out of greenery, fresh herbs, sticks and twigs. Or make several small arrangements (in shot glasses, salt shakers, glass jars) instead of one big centerpiece.

CANDLES: Candles provide instant mood enhancement. Take a couple of simple candlesticks, a cluster of votives or a group of various sizes and shapes. It's safest to stick with one color. You can wind ribbon through all the candles and flowers. (See Ribbon.)

MUSIC: Put soft dinner music on as you get ready. It will help you relax and entices yet another sense.

HOME DECOR

Do you have a dream of what you want your home to be? Do you see pictures in magazines that make you covet a certain look? Have you visited someone's home that makes you say to yourself "I want to *live* here." You need to pay attention to what it is about the house that makes you feel that way. For some it is a more Spartan, simple, ashram-like environment. For others it is a cluttered, cozy, trip down memory lane. You need to find out what makes your home fires burn.

Before you start planning, though, get real about what kind of home you want to maintain. Notice that the interior design photos in magazines never have clutter. If you live with stacks of stuff on every table, in every corner, you have to realize that redecorating will not change your personal habits. Create your design around what you are willing to maintain. (See Organization in Chapter 3.)

Judie: *As an interior designer, I had more than one client with a clutter problem. As we sat making their costly plans, I was forced to break it to them that their new kitchen would not be the dream they envisioned if they kept the piles of paper and cartons of stuff that lived on their countertops. In one case we brought in a home-organizing expert that did wonders with the clutter and designed a place in the garage for this mystery stuff. Things that they just couldn't do without were acknowledged and given a home. The rest was donated or thrown away!*

Sometimes investing money in an organizing service and/or professional cleaning crew can make as much difference as a new paint job. At least it gives you a clear idea of what you are working with. Once you have that, you can start brainstorming and making the changes you want.

When Judie was in high school she had an art teacher who told her class, "You will never have an idea that someone else hasn't already had. So find the masters who have come before you, that you like, and use them as your inspiration." In other words, plagiarize. We highly recommend it.

LAZYQUICK TIPS
The Idea File

Cut out pictures in catalogues, ads, magazines, newspapers. If there is something specific that you like in a picture, mark it with a pen. It could be just a style, fabric pattern or color, a piece of furniture or arrangement. Add color chips and fabric swatches. As you move along in the process, you can include room or furniture dimensions for shopping. Having an envelope or folder with pictures and ideas gives you a mobile design kit to help you plan and shop.

TASTE TEST

Let's talk. Do you like your taste? Do you think you know what good taste is? Taste is being peddled in every media image we see. The emphasis on creating a beautiful home has sky-rocketed. There are literally hundreds of magazines and catalogues fueling the "I want it, I need it for my home" mentality. Everyone's home is supposed to *exude* beauty. You should be able to drive by a house and salivate!

But, what if you don't feel confident in your taste? Or what if you know what you like, but you don't know how to create it? As with the Idea File, we encourage you to plagiarize, to adopt someone else's vision, to latch onto their taste and make it your own. Your own taste will develop gradually.

Judie: *When I was first married, I lived in a cookie cutter rental house that I was trying to make my own. In order to personalize the kitchen, I took the ironing board out of its little pocket cupboard and removed the door and made a spice cabinet. I put in several shelves and painted the inside with the latest colors: turquoise and acid green. To warm up the sterile bathroom, I bought my first wallpaper with a pattern of hanging beads in the equally current shades of hot pinks and oranges. In order to save time and money, I used the wainscoat approach and only papered from the sink level down. The pièce de resistance was the inch-wide hot pink braid I used to trim the top edge. I was so impressed with my efforts that I photographed my work and sent it in to the idea column in a woman's magazine. I was very disappointed when they didn't choose it.*

Several years later I looked at the photos I had sent in and was embarrassed by my bad taste. It was like those haircuts you see on yourself in old photos. "What was I thinking?" Now I see that this was all part of my evolution as a designer.

It's never too late to experiment with your taste. It's all grist for the taste mill. There really are no mistakes, because each thing you try gives you more information and experience for the future. Let yourself play with your taste… and in the meantime, plagiarize!

> *A little bad taste is like a nice splash of paprika. We all need a splash of bad taste – it's hearty, it's healthy, it's physical. I think we could use more of it, no taste is what I'm against.*

– Diana Vreeland, *D.V.*

COLOR YOUR WORLD

Color is the quickest, easiest way to change a room and also potentially the most problematic. It can be an overwhelming task if you walk into a paint store, see thousands of color chips and have no idea where to start. This is where the Idea File is essential. Clip and rip from every magazine where there is a picture of a room you like.

SORT BY COLOR. After you've got a good collection, sort them by color. Are they mostly pastels? Are they dark dramatics or cheery brights? If you see a trend, you've narrowed your choices. Even if you've got some of everything, don't worry because the next step will help you further narrow your options.

PREVIEW. What color can you live with? The same color that makes you feel good when it covers your body can drive you crazy when it covers your walls. The only sure way to know is to try it. Paint a large section of wall from floor to ceiling. Set different pieces of furniture and fabric samples in front of it and hang a favorite picture on it. See how you like the color at different times of day and night. Live with it for a while. If you love the color but it's too strong for a whole room, use it on furniture or window treatments and use a softer complimentary color on the walls.

COORDINATE YOUR COLORS. When you can see from one room into the next, you need to make sure that your colors work together. If you're going for contrast, make sure you have a balance and the colors complement each other.

PICK A COLOR, ANY COLOR

Color has been scientifically proven to affect our physical, psychological, and emotional health.

Moody Blues: Calm your nerves and soothe your soul.

Mellow Yellows: Feelin' good! Yellow tends to give us a sense of well-being and helps us function efficiently.

Radiant Reds: Invigorating. They stimulate action!

Gracious Greens: Warm and inviting. Mother Nature's favorite, after all.

SIMPLE SIMON DESIGN SENSE: THE TWO COLOR RULE

If you don't have confidence in your design choices – or you are looking for the easy answer – the best solution is to stay simple. For instance, you can't go wrong by designing around variations of just one color. The safest choice is always the neutral hues like whites, grays, or tans. You can mix fabrics, patterns, textures, and styles within the color range and still create a harmonious aesthetic.

Then, choose an accent color which you can add here and there, so when it's repeated around the room or house it excites the eye! Let's say you choose a yellow-green accent. A bowl of pears, a vase of flowers with bright green foliage, an accent table, lamp or throw pillows in that same green are small touches that can give the room a "complete" look.

You don't have to choose a second color. We've all seen pictures of the serene white beach houses that don't need any accent colors to feel fully designed. Pay attention to the details as you gather together the pieces, staying within your chosen hue, to create an interesting but uncluttered look. Note: pieces of stained wood furniture count as a color. So, either use stained pieces within your color palette or paint them (See Aging Furniture under Paint.)

SCINTILLATING SMALL SPACES

Whether you are dealing with a small apartment or house or you simply have a lot of small rooms, the Simple Simon Two Color Rule particularly applies to you.

Bridget had a three-room house with 90% of her square footage in one room. The kitchen and bathroom were separate, but everything else was in one space. Some might feel that she took the typical "paint every-thing white" approach. But, because she used one of her favorite colors as an accent, it was an appealing space. She also painted a few key pieces of wood furniture – the Lazy Woman's Way – i.e., four pieces in one hour!

Bridget: *The color I chose for my accent color was one that I've always loved – a deep purple-blue (in both bright and muted hues). I was inspired to bring it into my house after I saw a picture in a magazine of a dresser that color. It made my heart sing just to see it. When I went to paint my own furniture, I took the clipping to the paint store and matched it. Because the house was mostly white, I got to live with a color that excited me and still have my house be calm.*

THE WHOLE SHEBANG

Some of us become paralyzed at the thought of redoing a room, much less a whole house. Judie encourages her clients to think big, but start small. It's great to have an idea of the look you want to end up with, but it's easiest to decorate one step at a time. Wait until the walls are painted before you make the final choice on floors, fabric, or furniture. Having to redo your work is never lazy.

LAZYQUICK TIPS
Small Change –
Big Impact

Keep it simple and minimize stress by starting small. This can mean taking the only piece of furniture that you love, hanging a favorite picture or mirror over it, and crowning it with a bunch of flowers. When you have one place in your home that you love, it's refreshing. Beautiful homes are often born out a series of small changes like these.

RETIREMENT

If it doesn't please your eye, why have it around? When your taste has changed and you don't like things anymore, just be patient and slowly retire them.

REINCARNATION

You can give something a new life by using an old thing in a new way. Change where and how you use something. Turn an end table into a bed stand, a watering can into a vase, an old picnic hamper into a magazine basket next to your bed, a dining room table into a desk, or a tired entertainment center into your child's multi-purpose storage piece.

continued...

REFURBISHING

Give a table a whole new look with a Lazy Woman's Paint Job or cover it with a special vintage cloth. Change the knobs, or paint just the drawer fronts on a dresser. You don't have to spend hours or days with stencils and appliqués unless you love doing it.

FABRICS

Don't worry, we're not going to make you sew! But you can make an instant slipcover with a heavy sheet or tablecloth. They are pre-hemmed and big enough to cover some couches and most chairs. You can lay them over the piece like a throw or with a little effort, tuck-and-tie using ribbon and safety pins.

ACCENTS

When you clean up and move stuff around, try removing all the accents from the room. Put back the pieces that work together. Build on those accents, staying in the same color field with throws, pillows, candles, vases, etc.

PAINT

Both of us have loved paint since we were children. We love to play with it, so painting furniture in our houses is our idea of fun! If you were not born holding a paint brush, though, don't fret. Pick up the phone, call someone for a recommendation, book the painter, and go out and get your nails done. As Bridget's friend BJ says, "There are people for that!" Like cooking, gardening, sewing etc., if it makes you happy, go for it! If it burdens, oppresses, or depresses, take the easy way out.

X-RATED

PAINT & ENCLOSED SPACES

We learned the hard way once: you need ventilation – especially when spray painting. No matter how small the painting job, make sure you have plenty of fresh air. It's best to paint outdoors, but if you can't move the object outside, open windows and use fans. But, please avoid headaches, nausea, and brain damage – have plenty of air circulating. Also, of course, obey the manufacturer's instructions!

AGING: THE DESIGN MAVEN'S DELIGHT

While we are trying to keep *ourselves* from looking old, interior decorators are telling us that furniture and architectural accessories *should* look old. Here are some very quick solutions to making new stuff look vintage in a snap.

Refinishing Furniture:
The Lazy Woman's Furniture Paint Job

The Lazy Woman's Paint Job is neither labor-intensive nor time-consuming, and it doesn't require gathering up a lot of tools.

Use whatever paper or plastic (including market bags) you have on hand as drop cloths to minimize cleanup, grab your paint, a brush (if needed) and go for it! This can be a spur of the moment act to give you an instant change.

Use Spray Paint Whenever You Can

It comes in so many colors (don't limit yourself to paint stores, sometimes craft stores have an even better selection) and it comes in matte and satin finishes, which are what you need for furniture. It dries quickly, which makes it easy to finish a project in an hour. Spray **lightly**...again, **lightly**... because you can always add more! You can also use spray paint for highlights and accents by spraying directly into a pie tin and then brushing it on.

Don't Fret Over Flaws

Thank God the slightly imperfect look is in style. Just get the paint on and tackle any drips or gross imperfections with sandpaper when the piece is dry. Remember: you can always hide things with another light coat.

LAZYQUICK TIPS
Aging Furniture

Note: Make sure the furniture you are aging is NOT a valuable antique.

When aging, remember: **layers = years**. There are several shortcut techniques to create this look. The great thing about this is you can't really make a mistake, because taking paint off or putting paint on all helps create an aged look.

If you can move the furniture outside, choose a color spray paint (satin or matte finish.) **Spray lightly**, then sand, then maybe add a little more of the same or a different color, and then a little more sanding until you like the look.

If you are inside, take **quick-drying** acrylic paint and thin it with water to make a wash. Paint a little on and if it's too much, sand it off; if too little, do another layer.

Sometimes **sanding** alone does the trick. In all cases, sanding more on the corners, the edges, around the knobs – all the places that naturally wear – is what gives something a vintage look. To quickly create an aged look, just take a dark wood stain diluted with paint thinner, rub a layer on, leaving build-up in the grooves. Wipe and layer until it looks old.

continued...

Aging Metal

Metals age because of chemical reactions. For instance, copper rusts to a blue-green, steel rusts to red. Leaving things outside for the elements to rust and patina is a no-hassle approach. The **patina** and **rust kits** in the hardware store are fast and pretty darned easy. Some metal objects have a clear coating that will prevent the aging reaction, but if you sand to expose the metal, it will age where the coating has been scraped off.

Aging Pottery

Green Mossy Look: Paint pot with a thin layer of yogurt, beer, or a mixture of fertilizer and water, leave it in the shade and eventually you will get a mossy pot.

Paint Wash: Take any acrylic paint (watered down to watercolor consistency) in a neutral, whitewash or moss green color, and brush it on the pot with a rag. Play with the application and just stop when you get the effect you like.

Aging New Wood

To give new wood an **instant weathered look**, get powdered ferrous sulfate. (Look in the yellow pages under chemicals.) Add 1 teaspoon of ferrous sulfate powder to about 1 gallon of water. This can be brushed or sprayed depending on the size of the area. Within minutes your brand new birdhouse, garden fence, or mailbox looks 100 years old!

GARDEN

Most of us who garden feel like we want more time for it or are looking for shortcuts to make better use of our time. People who want to begin gardening are either unsure about where to begin or how to find time.

As evolving gardeners who can't stay out of the dirt, we have honed our skills through trial and error. We want a beautiful garden, but we do have day jobs. Our tips are aimed toward make gardening experiences simple, effective, and rewarding.

For those of you who have trouble seeing the connection between gardening and a lazy life, we offer a few words. Where else can you be in nature, get the double reward of work well done *and* a work-out, while getting so absorbed that cares and worries are banished? Gardening can happen, by the way, on your back porch or balcony too. Even a cluster of pots calls for watering, picking and pruning. It takes you outside and into another world.

> "Working in the garden...gives me a profound feeling of inner peace. Nothing here is in a hurry. There is no rush toward accomplishment, no blowing of trumpets. Here is the great mystery of life and growth. Everything is changing, growing, aiming at something, but silently, unboastfully, taking its time."
>
> – Ruth Stout, *How to Have a Green Thumb Without an Aching Back*

CULTIVATING GARDEN TIME

Whether it's *making time* or *saving time*, it all adds up to more garden time.

Keep your **tools** in a bucket/basket by the back door — gloves, clogs, clippers, fertilizer, etc. so you don't waste time gathering it all up.

Seduce your **partner** into joining. You don't have to beg for gardening time; offer a back rub or a movie as part of the deal.

Make a **kids'** area near your garden, so that you can garden while they play nearby. After a big rain, put them in their grubbiest clothes, set them down in a place that's mostly **weeds**, and let them pull, pull, pull. You take over in the areas where it's hard to tell the weeds from the flowers. It's most satisfying to pull weeds after a good rain.

A **soaker hose** allows you to slowly water a large area, keep the water off the foliage and avoid over-watering. You lay it down, turn it on low, and come back when it's done.

LAZYQUICK TIPS
Instant Garden-in-a-Pot

GET A POT: Choose one at least 12 inches in diameter because smaller pots need more frequent watering.

POTTING SOIL: Leave several inches between the top of the soil and the top edge of the pot so there's a well for water.

BUY PLANTS: Choose plants that take the same sun exposure and a similar amount of water to thrive. Read the tags or ask. Most nursery employees love to talk about plants. The textures, heights, and colors are up to you. Some people like the plants to be the same height; others like taller plants toward the middle or in the back, surrounded by lower plants. Ivy is always a good filler and will hang over the edge nicely.

PLANTING: Make sure the roots are not in a hard knot. If they are, loosen them a little with your fingers or tap them with a trowel. Start in the middle of the pot and work out, making sure all the plants are level.

WATER: Soak thoroughly when first planted. Then, if uncertain, underwater. If the soil is dry to the touch, it's time to water.

In a television interview, actress Anne Bancroft told a story about her obsession with the organic garden she started when her son was in school. She planted with passion and worked very hard. Her garden yielded bounteous and delicious crops. She loved it. But once her son went off to college, she promptly let it drop. It is now a lovely cutting garden, which she lets someone else tend. Gardens can be as consuming – and nurturing – as you want them to be.

MINI HERB GARDENS

Whether they're in the ground, in a window box or pot, alone or mixed in with flowers, fresh herbs take just about any meal from the mundane to the marvelous.

When you cut herbs back, put the clippings in a jar of water or tie them with a string and dry them on your window sill. Either way the sight and scent will be a treat. The herbs we've found the easiest to grow and use are: cilantro, basil, parsley, thyme, and, of course, rosemary and lavender. Mint and oregano should be grown in containers or they will invade surrounding plants and take over the whole area.

SHARING YOUR GARDEN

Using, sharing, and showing off your garden is the bonus. Not only do you get all that great therapeutic exercise from gardening, but you have a special place for family and friends to get together. A few patio chairs and a table or two – even if it's in an open bark-covered area – make for a gathering place. Throw in an umbrella, a couple of candles, a fountain, or some statuary and you have a sanctuary. For the Lazy Woman, of course, the most essential part of her garden is her hammock.

HANDS ON GARDEN PARTIES

Whether it's for your birthday or just to celebrate the season, a Hands On Garden Party is a great way to get some help in your garden and have a chance to entertain, too! Select some friends who are game for a little adventure. Tell them to wear their grubbies and come get down and dirty in your garden. If it's your birthday, let them bring plants as presents. Of course, refreshments are part of the deal, but it can be a lazy meal or snack. There's something special about sitting down to eat with someone after you've planted a bag of bulbs together. There's a sense of camaraderie and accomplishment that makes everyone glad they came. They get into the garden and enjoy wonderful company!

WARNING: READ LABELS

Pay attention to the size descriptions on plant tags. If you ignore these it can lead to the very un-lazy work of ripping plants out because they are crowding each other or covering paths.

LAZY WOMAN'S HEROINES:
LAVENDER & ROSEMARY

A lazy plant is one that needs little or no attention and little water. In most climates, lavender and rosemary grow like weeds with just about no effort. They are drought resistant, so you can literally forget to water them for quite a while and they will still yield bounteous crops.

INSTANT BOUQUETS AND GIFTS

Even if all you have in your garden is these two plants you can make a lovely, fragrant bouquet. Tie it on any present for a wonderful touch! It takes 5 seconds to grab several little blooms bunch them together, and tie with a bow. We promise, people will ooh and aah when they see your present with this one little embellishment.

FOOD DECORATION

Add a sprig of lavender or rosemary on a plate of food. Lavender is especially beautiful with fruit, and rosemary is wonderful with meats and vegetables. A little bunch of herbs and a few leaves with a slice of lemon or lime on top take a few seconds to make and bring beauty and elegance to any meal.

LAVENDER THE HEALER

Lavender is said to be good for the immune system. They're even putting it in mainstream products now – especially baby products. Having a little bouquet of lavender (whether dried or in water) next to your bed is not only a lovely fragrant addition to the bedroom, but may actually help you as you sleep.

ROSEMARY THE FLAVOR FRIEND

For roasted potatoes, drizzle with olive oil and sprinkle rosemary over cut up potatoes. Add salt and pepper. Roast at 400° until crispy and to your taste. Sprinkle lightly toasted rosemary on mashed potatoes or focaccia bread. Rub rosemary under the skin of your roasting chicken. Or, throw a couple teaspoons into your favorite bread recipe.

COMPOST

What does a Lazy Woman do with her garbage? The lazy answer can be to compost.

You may ask why a Lazy Woman would go to the effort of composting in her garden. Well, here are four darn good reasons:

1. You get a better nutrient-rich soil amendment – FREE!

2. Once you set up the system, it takes very little to get it to work for you! You can forget about it, and it will still be there when you want to start again. Often it's even richer and better when neglected. What else can you improve by ignoring it?

3. You feel good because you help save the planet.

4. Most important: you can feel OK about all the fruits and vegetables that accidentally rot!

Judie: *I have gone through times when I composted regularly and times when I haven't done it at all. I recently unearthed my old compost pile and started up again. For however long it lasts this go-'round, I'll enjoy it.*

LAZYQUICK TIPS
How to Compost

Buy a compost container, or just choose a corner of your garden and make a pile. You want to have the compost in as much **sun** as possible, so it will "**cook**". Try to alternate **layers** of browns and greens. When you add kitchen waste, dig it in or throw on a thin layer of dirt, so it doesn't attract flies. Keep a pitchfork nearby to **turn and stir** when you think of it. Water the pile occasionally keeping it moist but not soggy. Depending on the ingredients, the temperature, and how often you turn it, you will see that you are creating a black, moist, crumbly, **rich** compost. It's "done" when you can't recognize any of its ingredients. Use it to enrich your garden beds, lawn, or to make potting soil.

WHAT TO COMPOST

THE BROWNS
Dry leaves, grass clippings, bark chips, dryer and vacuum lint, limited amounts of cardboard and sawdust.

THE GREENS
Coffee grounds, tea bags, eggshells, rotten fruits and veggies, peelings, grass clippings, and green leaves.

WHAT NOT TO COMPOST

Dairy products, pet waste, nut shells, fish and meat scraps, bones, and cooked food.

LAUNDRY

Do you love looking in the linen closet, seeing beautifully folded towels and sheets, and smelling the fresh sweet smell of "clean"? You're lucky if laundry is your thing and you never end up with a pink something that used to be a pretty white something.

If you find it a drag and somehow can never seem to whittle down the mountain waiting to be washed, we're here to give you a little relief!

PREVENTATIVE LAUNDRY

Even if you love doing laundry, when life gets too hectic you need to pick up all the extra time that you can.

TOWELS: Towels can last longer if they get hung up properly so they dry out between uses.

SHEETS: Skip a week – most of us don't need to change the sheets weekly. If they don't feel fresh, try this quick pick-me-up: take a towel and hit the bottom sheet, dusting off any debris and then toss a few drops of scented oil on the pillows. Lavender is a particularly good option.

CLOTHES: When you get undressed, if you can wear it again, hang it up. Even laying it across a chair can do the trick. This is one of those cases where taking a minute now can save you many minutes in the future.

HOUSEHOLD LAUNDRY: Take a quick laundry survey through the bedrooms and bathrooms. Get kids and/or mates to hang up and pick up so they can use things again. If the culprit is not home, decide if it's worth it to leave things on the floor to make a point.

LAZYQUICK TIPS
Avoiding Laundry Mishaps

SEPARATING: This is the most important step. Separate by color first: make light, medium, and dark piles. Then separate the light-weight/synthetic/permanent press dark colors from heavy weight darks. Do the same for medium and light colored piles. Don't mix things that make lint (towels, flannel etc.) with things that attract lint (knits, corduroy, etc.)

READ LABELS: It's usually best to stick with the instructions on the label, but if you never get around to hand-washing things, you can try machine washing instead of letting things live forever on the bottom of the hamper! Do hand wash on gentle cycle in cold water with mild detergent. Or hand-wash and throw into washer for the gentle spin cycle – this is the quickest way.

LINE DRY/DRY FLAT: Most things can be thrown in a warm dryer for a few minutes then laid on a towel-covered flat surface or hung on a hanger to air dry. A few minutes in the dryer helps to smooth out any wrinkles left from wringing or spinning. These things usually need no ironing!

ONE-SECOND-SWEEP: Make sure the washer and dryer are completely empty before you throw stuff in. If you don't, you might end up with things mysteriously coming out of the wash splotched or "tie-dyed."

continued...

SOAP/STAIN REMOVERS/BLEACH/SOFTENERS: Try different products and pick your favorites. For kids' clothes or any heavily soiled items, a pre-soak can't be beat. If you don't have a laundry sink, use a plastic bucket. Overnight soaking can work wonders. Chlorine bleach can transform dingy whites but is hard on the fabric and the environment. The best bet is to use it only when necessary, diluting before adding. Always check fabrics for colorfastness. Fabric softeners are a matter of personal preference. They can help reduce static cling, and some people feel they make clothes softer and love the smell. Be careful with all additives, because people can be allergic to them.

Out, out damn'd spot!

– William Shakespeare

LAZYQUICK TIP
Spots and Stains

Treating the spot immediately with cool water – or soda water, if you have it – is a good first attack for any stain. Never use hot water, because it will set the stain.

On whites, diluted chlorine bleach takes out almost everything. On colors, try diluted bleach on a part of the lining to test. If there are just a few small spots, use a Q-tip to dab on the spots. Rinse with cold water.

BLOOD/HEAVY DIRT/GRASS/FOOD STAINS: Use a pre-soak product and warm (not hot) water.

INK: Saturate the spot with hair spray and rub with a clean cloth or rub with toothpaste until spot is gone. Launder as usual.

RED WINE: Wet the stain with cold water. Then rub table salt into the stain.

BLEACH STAINS: If bleach splashes on your favorite pants leaving a trail of white spots, permanent marking pens can be used for a great cover up. Art stores carry them in a huge range of colors.

The truly Lazy Woman carries Shoutwipes (Babywipes for stains). These are individually wrapped, so you can put them in your purse, car, etc.

QUICKIE LAUNDRY

The baseball game starts in 30 minutes and the uniform is dirty. You thought your "lucky" shirt was at the dry cleaners, but it's still in the hamper. Your dinner party is about to begin and you just spilled gravy on your top. What to do, what to do, what to do?

Hand wash and put in the washer for spin cycle only and then tumble dry! Yes, hand wash, rinse, spin and pop it in the dryer. If it's just a spot or a dribble, just spot clean and use a hair dryer. A hair dryer is also effective as a quick wrinkle remover. Use a light spritz of water for particularly tough wrinkles.

When you are doing a quickie hand wash, it doesn't mean it has to be gentle. You can get tough dirt out, too — just use stain removers, bleach, etc.

THE LAZY BEAUTY OF LAUNDROMATS

If you feel overwhelmed by the prospect of chipping away at the pile (or piles) of dirty laundry, try this: Pick a book or magazine and gather up all the change around your house. Pile the laundry into your car and drive it to the laundromat. Do all those loads at one time! Try to get the big, heavy-duty machines for the towels and sheets. Make it an adventure! Hit the vending machine and buy the orange soda or candy bar that you don't normally allow yourself. And, as you fold the last piece of laundry (which, by the way, feels so much easier at those big folding tables), applaud yourself for a job lazily done!

If even this is too much time or effort, take the piles to a "wash and fold" and come back to pick up your folded laundry. Sometimes it's worth the expense to catch up on undone laundry and get a fresh start!

CHAPTER ONE

CLEANING

"Gamma used to say, "Too much scrubbing takes the life right out of things..."

– Betty MacDonald, *The Egg and I*

Does this topic fill you with dread? Do you have issues left over from childhood? Were you the one who was expected to do most of the cleaning, or were you considered the slacker – the lazy sister – perhaps even called a "pig"?

Almost every woman we have talked to about cleaning has a story to tell. Whatever your baggage about cleaning is, carrying it with you as you vacuum only makes the work more difficult. Worse yet, if you let cleaning issues paralyze you, the housework piles up and becomes a Herculean task that takes so long that by the time you are finished, it's time to start all over. Often there are much deeper emotional reasons to avoid cleaning.

Judie: *I avoided cleaning as much as possible in my youth, preferring to doodle and daydream. In college, the Dean of Women sent someone in to photograph my dorm room and tried to penalize me for its unsanitary state. (Her previous position had been as head of a girls' reform school.) I was somewhat embarrassed, but having far too good a time to really care. Cleaning became more problematic for me when I married and had children. Then I felt overwhelmed and never managed to keep the house clean for very long. Just the thought of having to clean my house was enough to*

*keep me from getting out of bed. When I did get up, I knew
I would face puddles of juice and spilled Cheerios.*

*At this time, I had the great good fortune to have a next
door neighbor who was perhaps the first Lazy Woman
mentor in my life. She took me under her wing one morning when the kids and I arrived at her front door to borrow
milk for breakfast. She was warm and friendly and invited
us in. Her house was even messier than mine, but she did-
n't act embarrassed. She had no sense of pretense or discomfort and was immediately interested in me, my toddlers, and
especially my newborn. She took the baby in her arms, set
my two and four year olds down to play with her three and
five year olds, brushed the crumbs and cereal off a spot on
her kitchen table, told me to sit down and served me a cup
of tea. In the two and a half years we lived next door to
each other I never saw her turn down anyone's need because
she was too busy. This wasn't the end to my up and down
relationship with cleaning but it helped form what has
become my lazy philosophy toward homemaking and LIFE!*

If cleaning is your delight, then have at it and take
pity on the rest of us that are swimming upstream most of
the time. The Lazy Woman allows cleaning to take its
place in the rank and file of the necessities and responsibilities of life, while not allowing it to be a constant burden.

Before you even start cleaning: pause a moment to think about what you want to accomplish. Do you want to *straighten up* or do you want to *deep clean*? Judie spent years sabotaging her desire to have a more presentable house by getting sidetracked with deep cleaning. When the kitchen was a mess and there was only an hour before leaving to pick the kids up at school, she would end up cleaning the grout in the tile. The result was a double negative when everyone commented on the messy kitchen and no one noticed the clean tile.

THE BLITZ

Your mother-in-law calls and she's stopping by in fifteen minutes. Grab a couple of grocery bags and start at the front door. Put the toys, shoes, sweaters, mail – anything you want to keep – in one bag. Once the floor is clear of valuables, pick up any newspapers, popsicle sticks, or other trash, and shove it in the second bag. Scan the floor for any obvious dirt – lint, threads, leaves, etc. – and shove it in the trash bag. Check the furniture – plump the pillows, stack magazines neatly and add things to your bags as needed. Shut the bedroom doors. It helps to have those hotel DO NOT DISTURB signs on the doorknobs. Gather the dirty dishes in a sink filled with soapy water. Set your bucket of cleaning supplies on the counter and get out the mop and broom. After all, you've been interrupted just when you were starting to clean the kitchen!

X-RATED: CLEANING

"Bleach + Ammonia" *sounds* like it would make for a good cleaning duo, but this combination can do serious damage. The fumes are toxic. Never use them together.

LAZYQUICK TIPS
Seven Cinderella Shortcuts

1. PORTABLE PHONE WITH A HEADSET: You can pick-up, clean, empty the dishwasher and have a nice long chat with your mom or catch up with a friend.

2. CLEANING WIPES: Keep under the sink in bathrooms and kitchen. When company is arriving in 10 minutes, give the sink, counter and toilet a quick once over.

3. GATHERING BASKETS: Keep a decorative basket in each room. When you want to do a quick pick up, put the stuff that people leave around in it so they can retrieve things for themselves but meanwhile the room looks presentable.

4. TIDY TABLES: Clearing off tables or putting things in neat piles makes a room look cleaner.

5. SWEET SCENT: Keep a natural scented spray in each room for a clean smell.

6. MICROWAVE MAGIC: For easy microwave oven cleaning, microwave a bowl of water for five minutes, and splattered food will wipe right off.

7. SHOWER POWER: Spray one wall of the shower with tile cleaner before you enter shower so that it goes to work as you get ready. Then scrub it down when you get in…before you scrub you!

Do I Know You?

Nurturing Relationships Without Losing Yourself

Friendship

Neighbors

Dating

Sex

Romance

Marriage

Divorce

Composting Your Life

Compromise

INTRODUCTION

To be human is to be pulled in opposite directions – between the need to be independent and the need to be intimate. This is seen clearly in the toddler who throws tantrums when she doesn't get her way, but who cries for mommy when she is left at day care. Although not as dramatically clear in teenagers and adults, this yearning for someone to bond with is deep inside us all. We long for the nectar from these loving relationships. It's as if family, friends, neighbors, and lovers are each part of an enormous garden.

We want to cultivate our gardens and we want our gardening to nourish us. Sometimes it does, sometimes it doesn't. There are certainly some weeds we'd like to pluck, but that's not always possible. Then there are the flowers we'd like to control – we want the tulips to bloom in time for the party, the rose to climb in just such a way, the hydrangea to be the perfect shade of blue. This is what we want from friendships.

It's balancing these conflicting internal drives – to be in control and to be connected – that colors all of our relationships. It's hard to feel connected when you are annoyed by someone's opposing views. Ultimately, it is what makes the deepest or most intimate relationships the most difficult. In marriage, two people who each want their own way are supposed to come together and follow the same course. Well, how do you do this? The Lazy Woman's Way: use everything as compost.

The Lazy Woman's Garden of Relationships nourishes your soul. You may have to pull a few weeds from time to time, but it's possible to cultivate a beautiful garden.

" FRIENDSHIP

*If we listened to our intellect, we'd never
have a love affair. We'd never have a
friendship. We'd never go into business,
because we'd be cynical. Well, that's nonsense.
You've got to jump off cliffs all the time
and build your wings on your way down.*

– Ray Bradbury

Friendships, like romantic relationships, can push
your buttons, or fill your heart with love. The Lazy
Woman considers all relationships, whether intimate or
not, an opportunity to improve how she communicates
and to deepen her connections with others. Each
relationship offers us a chance to learn about ourselves
and how we relate to other people.

There are several issues that can come up around
friendships. Some of us have a hard time making
friends, some have trouble keeping them, and others
have trouble disentangling from unhealthy friendships.
Sometimes you struggle through hard times, just as you
do with family. Friendships take many forms and go
through cycles. Each friendship moves through your
life in a different way and brings with it its own set of
highs and lows.

For some people making friends is easy. For others,
moving to a new location, starting a new job, anything
that puts us in a situation where we have to make new
friends, creates anxiety.

LAZYQUICK TIPS
Making New Friends

START SMALL

It only takes getting to know one person to feel less anxious. Someone who recognizes you at the market, a meeting, the bookstore, can begin to make you feel at home.

KEEP COMING BACK!

The door to a friendship and potentially a group of friends may be just down the street. Drop by your neighborhood bookstore or cafe regularly. Even if you are really shy, you aren't out of luck, because most people who run those neighborhood businesses are friendly and inclusive.

FOLLOW YOUR INTERESTS

You can join a hiking club, book club, gym, church, etc. and meet people who share your interests. After a while, chances are you will develop friendships.

RELAX AND ENJOY

Go out to enjoy yourself! If you meet someone at a neighborhood concert, then so much the better. Try not to be attached to making a new friend. Otherwise, you're setting yourself up for disappointment.

NURTURING FRIENDSHIPS

It's never a bad time to tell a friend you appreciate them. Send a card that reminds you of them. Pick up the phone and tell them how much you appreciated the advice they gave you or the way they handled the PTA meeting. Express your appreciation. Acknowledge their contribution to your life.

SUSTAINING FRIENDSHIPS

If you notice you have difficulty sustaining friendships, it might be time for a little "Needs Assessment".

- Are you a high-maintenance friend?
- Are all phone calls from you laden with heavy problems or high drama?
- Do you flake on your friends, not return calls or not show up?
- Is friendship with you a one way street?
- Are you so needy that eventually your friends have to take a break from you to renew their own energy?
- Are you jealous of everything they gain and driven to compete or put them down?

If you identify with any of these questions, ask a family member or friend to help you assess what might be hindering your friendships. Listen to what they say and try not to get defensive.

DIFFICULT OR TOXIC FRIENDSHIPS

Sometimes you make a new friend and realize almost immediately that the friendship is taking a toll on you emotionally, financially, and/or physically. Sometimes it takes years before you wake up and realize this friendship has entered the Toxic Zone!

If you are trying to figure out whether someone is a toxic friend, use the "Needs Assessment" questions from above and turn them around. Are all their phone calls laden with heavy problems or high drama?

Often, these friendships can be shifted with some candid conversation. Ideally, the person will be open to discussing things, even if time has to pass before they can talk about it.

Other times, talking doesn't seem to help. If you've tried in the past to talk with a friend about the same issue only to be met with resistance on their part, it probably won't change things to keep mentioning it. It will only create more work and stress in the end. You need to decide if the friendship is worth keeping. If it is, know that reacting to their "stuff" just reinforces their behavior. When you stop, they'll either find someone else to mistreat or at least try a new tactic.

If any discussion causes the other person to slam the door in your face, it may mean that the friendship is really toxic, and despite any pain it causes you, your life will be easier without them.

EBBS AND FLOWS OF FRIENDSHIPS

All relationships ebb and flow. Over-analyzing and comparing friendships is not the Lazy Woman's Way. Allowing friends to pull back when they need to without taking it personally and accepting that sometimes they will be too busy to include you in their plans is all part of having realistic expectations. There will also be times when friends are needier or cling too long. In either case, try to remember Lazy Woman's Commandment #7, "You are a separate person," and detach.

NEIGHBORS

At times in your life, relationships with neighbors can be almost as strong as family relationships. Particularly if you have children, neighbors can become a large part of your support system. When this is the case, any difficulty or breach can be very traumatic for the whole family. Disagreements between the parents can end up affecting the kids and vice versa.

Other neighborly relationships range from this level of intensity to a non-relationship, where you never see each other, much less speak. You can have problems or issues with neighbors, though, even if you don't really know them.

"It's easier to love humanity as a whole than to love one's neighbor."

– Eric Hoffer

You might share the street, sidewalk – even a fence – but they can be a complete stranger. When differences arise you have no idea what's going on inside their heart or head, or what they're facing in their life. You never know why someone reacts the way he does. The only thing you can do is to be aware of how you respond.

Bridget had a much-delayed miracle with a neighbor she hardly knew. Three years ago a neighbor berated her for not keeping her dog in her own yard. Bridget wrote a sincerely apologetic note, but never heard a word back. Recently, she found a letter in her mailbox from that neighbor apologizing for her overreaction, admitting that she had kept Bridget's note all that time, with the intention of writing this apology.

Once you've done what you can do, just step back emotionally and know that it is the other person's problem. You don't have to wait for him to see the light to release the tension in your own life. It's amazing what happens when you let go of needing to be right. Remember Lazy Woman's Commandment #5, "You can either be right or be happy".

LAZYQUICK TIPS
Neighborly Relations in Troubled Waters

"I'M SORRY THIS BOTHERS YOU."

Even if you're not sure what you've done, you can calm troubled waters with "I'm sorry you thought I was insulting you" or "I'm sorry you think my dog barks too much," etc. You don't have to admit any wrong-doing, but say, "I'm sorry this bothers you." The first couple of times it might choke in your throat, but if you can, it may be enough to smooth things over.

LAY LOW

If you can't bring yourself to apologize or your apology is rejected, it may be best to just lay low. For instance, if a neighbor comes out of left field with something, which you can't even address or help solve, it might be best to do nothing and agree to disagree.

BRIBES AND PEACE OFFERINGS

Sometimes they are genuine, sometimes calculated, and sometimes a bit of both. Don't waste time pondering whether it's genuine or not. Sometimes a simple note alone will do, or perhaps a box of candy or bottle of wine can do wonders to mend neighborly fences. Again, you don't need to agree with them, just tell them that you're sorry they're upset.

DATING

No date is a waste for a Lazy Woman. You are always practicing your skills of communication, commitment, and intimacy. Your date is a "Practice Person."

Judie: *I've been with my Practice Person for over 35 years. Even though I sometimes think, "This could not be my soulmate" when we disagree, I see that my husband has taught me a lot of the lessons I came here to learn. Some of the lessons are unpleasant, yet we keep going, keep learning. That's how you get to the good stuff.*

If your date is your practice person for one night, one month, seven years, or whatever length of time, it is never a waste, because it's all about practicing. Nobody gets the relationship thing right every day. We just keep practicing.

When it comes to blind dates in particular, Bridget says "I go out to make a friend, and if it becomes more, that's great. But, I can also 'shop' for my other single friends. Maybe this person isn't right for me, but what fun to find someone for a friend."

The expectations about a single date can be so high. And everyone has her own piece of advice to share with you – *rules* about how to date, how to flirt, when to call, when not to call, how long to wait (girl time vs. boy time), when to write him off, etc. It's difficult, but necessary, to put all of this aside. Know that there are no mistakes and shoot from the hip; go from your gut. You have to do what works for you. If he's supposed to be your one and only, you can't scare him away. How very un-lazy it is to second guess how you are supposed to act and react to get a man!

> *"...nowadays what you want to do is make*
> *sure you know the difference between a*
> *flirtatious five-second eye contact and*
> *a psychotic stare. My rule of thumb is the*
> *five-second eye contact: if the person giving*
> *it to you is accumulating beads of*
> *perspiration anywhere on their body,*
> *don't give him your phone number,*
> *<u>don't</u> give him your phone number."*

– Merrill Markoe

The moral of the story: stay safe but have fun and don't worry. *Every* date is a success. Practice, practice, practice!

SEX

Sex is a highly charged word. It's probably the hottest topic in our social discourse. One of the most popular shows on TV, HBO's "Sex and the City" centers almost entirely on women and their sex lives. Men watch it to try to figure us out and women watch it, in part, to know that they aren't alone, or in some cases, to live vicariously through the characters. We all have our own judgments about topics surrounding sex: when to have it, how often, for how long, which positions to try, which taboos to respect, etc.

We need to keep sex in perspective as part of the human condition, ideally as something to be connected with love, intimacy and positive experiences. But on the practical side, having or not having sexual relationships is something you need to decide for yourself.

> *Of all the things that human beings did together, the sexual act was the one with the most various of reasons.*

– P.D. James

Finding your own "sexual comfort zone" is crucial for the Lazy Woman. Otherwise, sex becomes a burden. It doesn't matter if you are married or single – you need to get to a place where your sex life feels right to you.

SEXUAL COMFORT ZONE METER

You have to customize your sexual behavior to your own inner voice. Only you can decide who, what, when, where, why or why not. Developing an awareness of your Sexual Comfort Zone is imperative to your well being. Here are some questions to help you clarify this.

MARRIED AND LONG-TERM MONOGAMOUS RELATIONSHIP

• Does it feel good? Are you having sex that's not satisfying to you? You need to strike a balance between meeting your physical needs and honoring your feelings about the role sex plays in your relationship.

• Do you use sex as a bartering chip? To manipulate? Is it a duty? Does it make you feel guilty? If sex has become a burden, that's not lazy. Try to step aside and leave all the judgments or resentments that you have about your partner (or you believe they have about you) outside the bedroom. Share a wonderful release and approach the relationship with a fresh and more loving attitude.

• Are you sexually shutdown? If you are avoiding any sexual issue, it ends up costing you on some level. It may not be conscious, but it's on the back burner...scorching. If this is painful for you to look at, you may need professional help.

continued...

SEXUAL COMFORT ZONE METER

SINGLE & DATING

• Does it feel right? Honor your feelings about the role sex plays in your relationship.

• Are you shutdown, or is there something that keeps you from having sex or leads you to have it compulsively? There is a Twelve-Step Program available if your sexual behavior is obsessive or compulsive.

• Do you use sex to get dates? Or attention? Does it make you feel guilty? Does the way you use sex cause problems in your life?

• Ask yourself the following questions: Who – someone you trust? What – an act you are comfortable with? Where – a safe place? Why – a healthy, non-compulsive reason? How – Are you practicing safe sex?

SINGLE & NOT DATING

• Are you self-gratifying? Are you missing the satisfaction of orgasm? When you crave sexual release, arrange a way to meet your needs. If this means candles and a bubble bath, then go for it. If you need inspiration, seek it out in books or films.

• If for cultural or generational reasons you are not comfortable masturbating, then accept that about yourself and don't feel guilty. You may find yourself investigating some of the literature available about celibacy. Celibacy is practiced by many happy people!

LAZYQUICK TIP
ORGASM

THE VIBRATOR
(FOR USE WITH OR WITHOUT A MATE)

Whether sex with your mate needs a lift, you want to spice up the bedroom, or you need a quick orgasmic fix when alone, vibrators are the Lazy Woman's answer. You don't have to enter a sex shop to get one either. You can go to the local drugstore and get a massager that will do the trick. Also, there is a great company called Good Vibrations in San Francisco that will send you a plainly wrapped catalogue, from which you can order many different playful and very satisfying toys.

THE SEX SHOP

Let the good times roll! Relax, it's only a store. Times have changed, sex shops have come out of the closet. Of course, there will be toys there that aren't your style. But what do you have to lose? An adventurous trip to a sex shop can be a great way to loosen inhibitions and get new ideas to try in bed. If it does nothing more than aid in removing embarrassing feelings about sex, it's worth it. And if you're worried that someone you know will see you – chances are they've been there too.

SAFE: THE SEXY LAZY WAY

Perhaps the most essential tip relating sex and a lazy life is the one that reminds you to put protection from pregnancy and STDs at the forefront of your mind. Whether it is with your mate or your date, you must be the one to protect yourself. Your life is never made easier by having to deal with an unwanted pregnancy or a life-altering disease. The technology is here. From IUDs to patches to cervical caps to the state of the art "pill," there's a lazy solution for everyone's lifestyle. If you are going to have sexual relations, make sure you are well protected.

ROMANCE

" And what's romance? Usually, a nice
little tale where you have everything
As You Like It, where rain never
wets your jacket and gnats never bite
your nose and it's always daisy-time. "

– D. H. Lawrence

If your definition of romance is someone else doing something thoughtful or sweet for you, and that person has to be a certain someone else, then you may be setting yourself up to feel deprived. Your partner probably doesn't score the same on the Romance Meter as you do. Many women complain that there's just not enough romance in their lives. We say "give it up!" We don't mean give up the desire for romance, just expand your definition.

You can make yourself feel more romantic by bringing beauty into your life. Remember to treat yourself to fresh flowers. Put on beautiful music. Light a scented candle or incense. Sit by the fire with a cup of tea, even if you've just got ten minutes. Book a pedicure or a massage. Buy something that makes you feel a little indulgent, like a new perfume or a more expensive piece of clothing. The important thing is to do it consciously, with the intention of creating romance. Let yourself feel pampered. Give yourself attention.

Another lazy solution to feeling under-romanced is to make sure that you get enough romantic moments with your mate. Don't be coy. Don't sit around dropping hints and waiting for him to suggest a romantic evening. Choose the movie that you think will be romantic and ask him to be your date. Let him know you're looking for a little romance and he's your #1 choice. Even the most unromantic mate will be flattered and won't be able to turn you down. It doesn't matter who sparks the fire, just so long as it gets lit.

LAZYQUICK TIPS
Romance for Two

BOOK A MASSAGE FOR YOU OR YOUR MATE

Have the masseur or masseuse come to your house so that after the massage you don't have to break the spell.

TREATS

Buy him his favorite cookies, ice cream, wine, etc. that he doesn't usually allow himself to indulge in… take the time to share the surprise with him!

POST-ITS

Yet another reason to have them always on hand…leave a little Post-it on his steering wheel or in his underwear drawer to remind him you love him. It takes 3 seconds to write and you might end up with 3 hours of his time!

CANDLES AND BATHS

Is your bathtub big enough for two? Prepare a candle-light bath and invite him in…Or, if it's not, pull up a chair while your mate enjoys a nice bath. Sometimes just bringing candles into the bedroom or bath can be a wonderful mood-enhancer.

FULFILL A WISH

We all have our wishes of what we'd like our mate to do for us. What's your mate's wish? If you don't know, ask him or have someone else ask him so you can surprise him.

MARRIAGE

To marry or not to marry, that is the question. Or is it who to marry, or how to find someone to marry? To stay married or not to stay married? The times of living contently, married or single, are woven together with times when nagging questions dominate your life: the "if only I was (wasn't) married, I would be happy" attitude. (See If Only in Chapter 7.)

Questioning your marital status on a regular basis is a sure sign of discontent, but it isn't necessarily rooted in marriage. Try to let go of the idea that marrying or divorcing will be the answer. Maybe you will marry or divorce, but either way, obsessing about your marital status won't help. Focus on what is before you right now, the mundane to the magnificent, and you will spend the time getting to whatever decision with a lot more joy in your daily life.

IT LOOKS SO EASY

Going from the romance of courtship to the reality of marriage is an adjustment for every couple even if they've lived together before the marriage. There is a certain level of deceiving oneself that exists in everyone's assumptions about what marriage will be like. You can't help but think "that will change when we're married" or "this doesn't really bother me." It's as if, out of the blue, within minutes of making the decision to marry, a veil falls over your eyes, slightly obscuring your view of reality.

> *Marriage is like twirling a baton,*
> *turning a handspring or eating with*
> *chopsticks; it looks so easy until you try it.*

– Helen Rowland, *Reflections of a Bachelor Girl*, 1909

Knowing *how* to be married does not just appear on your mind's radar screen when you say "I do." As with parenting, it is a "learn by doing" skill. Yes, you can read books, consult experts, and listen to friends and relatives, but essentially it is a trial and error business, with some of the best learning coming as a result of the most difficult situations. Everyone seems to be an expert. Sometimes the advice of others who have been there is helpful, but just as often it merely adds to the confusion. Since every person has an entirely different point of view on everything, and marriage involves two people trying to go through life together, there is plenty of room for conflict. Add the in-laws, children, step-children, friends, co-workers, experts, talk show hosts, magazine articles, TV, movies, career pressures, personal growth, sickness and health, richer and poorer…and it can break a marriage.

> *The best marriages, like the best lives,*
> *were both happy and unhappy.*
> *There was a kind of necessary tension,*
> *a certain tautness between the partners that*
> *gave the marriage strength, like the tautness*
> *of a full sail. You went forward on it.*

– Anne Morrow Lindbergh

Accepting that there is conflict in marriage, that it's OK to disagree, releases you from the burden of having to fix things. Even if your partner gets stuck in having to be right, you can step back and let go of having all the answers. This will open the door just enough for compromise.

Remind yourself, over and over again when necessary: "You are a separate person" (Lazy Woman's Commandment #7). You can love someone, want a different life for them, see they are burdened with problems or emotional difficulties, but *you cannot live their life* for them. When you really *get* that, it unplugs you from the fear you feel when you are not in sync or you can't fix their problems or make them feel better. This detachment makes your life easier, and brings an inner calm that feeds your relationship. Even if you can only detach for moments at a time, the more you practice, the more moments you will be able to string together. This kind of loving detachment creates a general sense of peace and contentment. It allows you the necessary distance to love someone for who they are, as they are, and not for what you want them to be.

> **"**O*nce the realization is accepted*
> *that even between the closest of human*
> *beings infinite distances continue*
> *to exist, a wonderful living side by*
> *side can grow up, if they succeed in*
> *loving the distance between them*
> *which makes it possible for each*
> *to see the other whole against the sky.***"**
>
> – Rainer Maria Rilke

DIVORCE

"Divorce is only less painful than the need for divorce."

– Jane O'Reilly

Is there anything that could ever make divorce effortless? Absolutely not! There are, however things you can do to make it more or less difficult. Divorce is a loss even if you are the one to initiate it. It signals a letting go of your dreams about your marriage. It means a change in your home, family, and lifestyle. When you add to this the deep emotions of hurt, blame, fear, anger and so on, the experience ranges from challenging to devastating.

There is nothing you can do to change many of these things. There is something, however, that you can do that will make everything different. This powerful tool is, of course, changing your attitude about your divorce. If you are the one who wanted the divorce it is often easier to "look on the bright side." But even then, there are moments when you may doubt your decision. If you are the one who was "left" it is often difficult to see the silver lining.

Judie: As we are writing this book I have two friends going through divorces. Many years and several children into their marriages their partners said they wanted out. The women were shocked but when they began to look back they both saw signs that they had been ignoring. How these women are dealing with their lives – estranged husbands, sad/mad children, plans for the future, and emotional reactions – is very different. What I notice each time I talk to them is, however, similar in one aspect. They are both moving from one stage to another, progressing, in their own way, and gaining strength and insight. With each hurdle – moving, custody arrangements, career plans, getting settled in a new routine – there is new found hope. Yes, there are still days when they fall into anger or self-pity, but neither of them stays there. Within four months, one of them has started culinary school and is on the way to her dream of being a chef, and the other has stayed in her same job but has gone from being the betrayed wife to having a new sense of completeness as a single person.

For both of these women there are still bad days and difficult times ahead. Just as when grieving for any loss, it is a day by day, moment by moment choice not to get sucked into self-pity and blame that makes all the difference. It may be that the best you can manage is to get out of bed in the morning, get dressed, and put one foot in front of the other. Ease up on yourself, and if you have kids, cut them some slack. The laundry and lessons aren't going to go away.

If ever there was a time to make sure you connect with family and friends – circle the wagons, so to speak – this is it. When you are drowning in judgment and fear, you can't really be present in your own life or for your children. Do whatever it takes – therapy, a support group, meditation – to get out of your head and back into your whole being. Divorce leaves no one unchanged. Whether or not it ends up being a catalyst for growth or becomes the cause of all your future woes is up to you.

Whenever I date a guy, I think, is this the man I want my children to spend their weekends with?

– Rita Rudner

For women with children, the option of moving on with your life is more complex. Even if the father totally leaves the picture you will be dealing with the emotional fall-out on your kids. If there is some form of shared custody or visitation, there will be ongoing contact. (See Parenting in Chapter 4.) Just as with the adults involved, your children's lives are forever changed by divorce. Whether this becomes a defining negative influence in their lives or a difficult but instructive part, is a matter of helping them choose, over and over again, to let go of blame.

Bridget: *My parents were divorced when I was 7, a precarious age (I later heard from psychologists) to be separated from Dad. There was a lot that wasn't great about it – mostly miscommunications and misunderstandings resulting from distance – but it formed who I am today and if I went back to undo that one thing…the rest of the story would fall apart and be rewritten. I wouldn't be writing this very sentence. Divorce, though, also made me see my mother as a truly independent woman, an independence she certainly would not have developed married to my dad. I'm sure this has a lot to do with my own fierce independence, which gave me the courage to be an entrepreneur, follow my own instincts, and try to make my own dreams come true. It also made me incredibly scared of people disappearing on me – not a fun by-product – but, again, a part of the whole.*

COMPOSTING YOUR LIFE

"Composting" is when the past fertilizes the future, when you take stuff that you thought was useless, a mistake, or rotten, and turn it into something useful, helpful, and fertile. We all have parts of ourselves, events from our past, that we think are "trash," that we either want to ignore or deny.

There are no mistakes in composting, nothing to be ashamed of, guilty about. We might as well admit that the events in our lives become a part of us, sit in us, resonating inside. If we aren't afraid of learning from the negative stuff, we might just transform it into something positive. There is neither good nor bad compost, only rich, richer, and even richer.

The *trick* is that you have to be aware and accept what happens in order to learn from it, to get some good fertile soil out of it. The *trap* is when you only blame and bitch about your trials and tribulations. Then you just... well, draw flies.

COMPOSTING AS AN ATTITUDE

If your way of thinking is "Aaaah, it's not finished, and that's OK" or "I don't have to know all the answers," then whatever you are experiencing all becomes part of the compost of your life. (See *Perfectionism* in Chapter 7.) You become wiser through the experience, not fixated on past disappointments or worried about future outcomes. You become engaged in the present. The same things are happening in your life, but they affect you differently if you are really living life as a "work in progress."

COMPROMISE

Compromise is a favorite Lazy Woman's tool, because it takes less time and effort than trying to win a battle – and the emotional damage is minimized! Years ago Judie and her husband found an artist that they both loved and decided they would buy one of his pieces. Unfortunately, they couldn't agree on which one. Since it was a large investment, the only way to resolve it was to choose a painting that was neither one's first choice. It took a lengthy heated debate, a lot of negotiating, and several trips to the gallery, but they finally found a piece both of them could appreciate. Judie and Jay still enjoy their painting – and the story behind it!

In some cases, compromise is just the beginning of moving toward a permanent solution. For instance, let's say you have to decide whether to put an elderly relative in a rest home. Family members can have opinions ranging from putting them in the home today to never allowing it. When you are stuck like this, you need to find a starting place. This could mean researching quality facilities, in-home care options, or just making a call to someone who has dealt with a similar situation. The compromise doesn't have to be the answer, but it can at least get you started. Usually taking one step opens the door to a solution.

The ability to compromise will help you move through life with more ease – from small issues like which movie to see to larger decisions like which house to buy. When you are starting at opposite poles, however, it's hard to see the compromise. Hopefully these few tips will get you on your way.

LAZYQUICK TIPS
Moving Toward the Lazy Middle Ground

GET CLEAR ON THE OPTIONS

If you need to, write down the options – even putting the opposing views on opposite sides of the page.

OPEN YOUR MIND AND HEART

Let everyone have a voice and offer even the wackiest of solutions. Sometimes the silliest ideas have the seed of an answer. Try to keep it as light as possible.

PIECES OF THE PUZZLE

Allow yourselves to agree on one aspect of the issue at hand. You may not solve the entire problem in one sitting. Sometimes breaking down the issue into parts can at least put you on the path toward resolution.

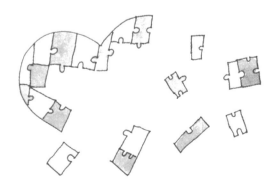

The Most Satisfying of Tools

EQUIPPING YOURSELF FOR A LIFE OF EASE

Organization

The Lazy Woman's Top Ten Tools

INTRODUCTION

When you hear someone say "I can't function unless I'm completely organized," or "I'm so unorganized I spend half my time looking for things," you know that a lot of her time and energy is going into organization. The Lazy Woman's approach is to tailor organization to one's own personal style. Even if you are a last-minute, shoot-from-the-hip kinda gal, your life will be easier if you take some time to organize.

You don't want to waste a lot of time spinning your wheels looking for lost items, arriving at stores without the things you wanted to return, or incurring late payments because you've misplaced your bills. On the other hand, being driven by a need to control every detail is exhausting.

There are some tools that make organizing and quick repairs easily doable. You need to have tools handy that do exactly what you want. Lazy Women gotta love those tools! Even if you think you're not a doer or a fixer, there are certain gadgets that with little effort will make your life easier. Our favorites come with a minimal learning curve, take relatively no space or maintenance, and are usually multi-functional.

ORGANIZATION

Some of us wait until our lives are an utter mess before we realize that we need to organize. Others organize regularly like seasonal cleaning. If you've let things get out of hand, don't take on too much. That's the surest way to get nothing done. Tackle large organizing jobs in small pieces, so you feel a sense of accomplishment when you finish each phase. Otherwise you will be depressed and quit, which is not lazy! If you are paralyzed and don't know where to start, you may need help. Sometimes you just can't see the forest through your own trees. You enter the office (closet, bedroom, etc.) to start, your eyes glaze over and you walk out. If you are one of these people, enlist an organizing buddy or hire someone. Make sure that your buddy is more brutal with editing your "stuff" than you are.

Judie's mom, Kay, is such an organizing freak that she not only organizes for family and friends, but now she is even being approached by friends of friends who have heard of her wondrous talent. Needless to say, Judie feels very blessed.

The bad news is that organizing has to be redone every once in a while. The good news is that you can rediscover stuff you forgot you had, reorganize things in a way that is new and exciting, and never run out of things to do in front of the TV.

LAZYQUICK TIPS
Organization Tools

CANVAS TOTE BAGS

Use these to schlep stuff. Often you get them free at promotional events, and you don't know what to do with them. Well, use them to get things back where they belong.

BASKETS

Use in each room as decorative containers for toys, magazines, as a catchall for quick pick-ups.

STORAGE BOXES (CARDBOARD OR PLASTIC)

We prefer plastic because they are more durable and you can see what's in them. Always label them, e.g., Summer Clothes, Tax Receipts, Christmas Decorations.

LABELS

Have a package of large labels on hand. You can always cut them to size if working with smaller boxes. They can double for address labels on mailing envelopes and boxes too.

RUBBER BANDS/PAPER CLIPS/TWIST TIES/STAPLERS/TAPE

Use these to group together miscellaneous loose stuff.

continued...

SHARPIES

We use the fine point for labeling. They are also great for labeling kid's lunch boxes, clothes, cups, water bottles, etc. because they are permanent on just about every surface.

POST-ITS

When you're overwhelmed by backed-up filing, take your unwieldy piles of paperwork into a room with clear floor space. Lay the filing on the floor by subject: health insurance, car insurance, taxes, etc. Put a post-it below it. Don't leave anything unlabeled – come up with a title that makes sense, even if it seems ridiculous at first. Play with the categories until you find the most sensible name and place for every piece of filing you have. Then you are ready for the files!

BACKPACKS

Extra kids' backpacks can be great storage/organizing tools for kids' toys. You can have one that specifically goes to and from the car with kids' stuff. You deal with the mess and conveniently transport the stuff.

BASKETS/DRAWERS/DECORATIVE CONTAINERS

Keep tools that are often used together in something portable so you can carry them from room to room.

GIFTS: gift wrap, ribbon, card, tape, scissors, etc.

MAILING CENTER: stamps, envelopes, pens, tape, etc.

BASIC TOOLS: hammer, screwdriver, nails, etc.

LAZYQUICK TIPS
Organizing Techniques

CLOTHES CLOSET

Do you wear it or don't you? Sort through and take out the things you don't wear. If you're not ready to part with them forever, box them and get them out of your closet (i.e. to the garage or storage). After a while, the clothes may end up going to a thrift shop without your having to even look through the box. At the very least, you won't have to paw through as much when you get dressed.

OFFICE/PAPERWORK

UNDECIDED BOX: Same theory as the closet; take unimportant papers that you can't part with, box them and store in a closet. You can go back later, but you won't get sidetracked and totally abort the whole process by starting to read old mail, etc. They're around if you need them, but they aren't cluttering your workspace.

BULLETIN BOARD: This is a good tool for the little pieces of paper and business cards that you don't have time to file away. A bulletin board can hold things that you might otherwise lose. There are many painted, framed ones that are aesthetically pleasing.

FILES: If you can, have a file cabinet. If not, use a box. Filing doesn't have to be done all at once. Just keep

continued...

your stack in a box marked "papers to be filed." If being alone with all that paper is daunting, take it out when you are watching TV or at least put on some fun music and make a cup of tea while you sort!

WHOLE HOUSE

ORGANIZING TOTES: Have traveling baskets or canvas tote bags to move things from your house to your car, from work to home, from one room to another. If you have an upstairs or a large house, this is especially important. Otherwise you end up going back and forth over the same ground, trying to get stuff where it belongs. For instance, by having a "Car Bag" (that goes only from house to car), where kids can put their homework, lunch, ballet clothes, etc. you can teach them about responsibility and help keep your house picked up.

KEYS/PURSES/LEASHES/KIDS' BACKPACKS: Identify a place and stick with it. You can use a bowl, a small basket, a cachepot, an entry table, shelf, or hook.

KIDS' STUFF

BACKPACKS: Kids can develop the habit of putting their own stuff for school or overnight trips into their back-packs.

TOY CONTAINERS: Whether it's a toy box or basket, even toddlers can learn to put their toys in a box and get them off the floor. Have one in the family room and/or kitchen, too. Even if your kids don't do it, it gives you a place to shove it!

THE LAZY WOMAN'S TOP TEN TOOLS

If you've never used any of the The Lazy Woman's Top Ten Tools, you may want to try them out. We use them all on a regular basis and are here to extol their benefits! If they sound good to you, give them a try.

1. LAZY WOMAN FASTENERS

VELCRO: This versatile invention can be sewn on cloth as a quick fix for a duvet cover with missing buttons, for making removable pillow covers, fastening a slipcover to a piece of furniture or to make any number of projects easier.

Think Velcro, though, not just for sewing needs, but when you are trying to attach things in different applications. Use the adhesive backed Velcro when repairing luggage and purses. It's also great for affixing lightweight objects to the sides of cabinets, computers, shelves, etc.

GLORIOUS GLUE: Glue makes almost any fix-it or craft job easier. It's just a matter of having the right glue. The lazy thing is that it doesn't cost much, take up much space, or involve having a high level of skill. You have to know which glue to use for which application, but usually the container gives you a pretty clear list of do's and dont's. Even if you aren't much of a hands on person, the right glue can convert you, or at least help you out in a pinch.

LAZYQUICK TIPS
The Wacky Wonderful World of Glue

Glue is under-appreciated. These are some of the friendliest, laziest, and hardest working glues on the market. Don't be daunted by the large selection. These are all no-brainers to use.

TACKY CRAFT GLUE

This glue comes in a consistency thicker and stickier than ordinary white glue. It's not as runny, so it can be more selectively applied.

SUPER/KRAZY GLUES

When these work, they really, really work – even on your fingers. The dried glue, by the way, can be taken off your skin with nail polish remover.

GLUE STICK

Not just the friend of children, they are unbelievably quick and easy to use with paper.

RUBBER CEMENT

For large paper areas, this is preferable to a glue stick because it's so easy to paint on, but it is generally interchangeable with a glue stick.

SPRAY ADHESIVE: There's nothing faster when attaching two paper items – paper to paper, photos to cardboard, paper to cardboard. Just spray and attach!

Also, you can use it for crafts to quickly cover large areas – potpourri to topiaries, silk or dried flowers to styrofoam forms, moss to baskets, etc.

2. THE ALMIGHTY GLUE GUN

This is the ultimate choice for any tough job that can take the heat. You can easily position the glue, it holds heavily weighted things together in seconds and dries clear. Glue guns start at under $5 and they'll save you hours of time and frustration. Both the authors have a *few* glue guns in their craft arsenal!

Warning: Don't touch the hot glue or the tip of the gun... We speak from experience.

3. POST–ITS

Post-its are great for reminders and organization. They also make for an easy message system. You can take a post-it and stick it to a cup, computer, door, phone, etc.

When children have to do research for school you can add an element of fun by using post-its for markers.

Bridget has been accused of perhaps overusing post-its. A friend once suggested that she put one on her door with the word "open" on it. But the same friend loves it when she uses a post-it system of reminders on her refrigerator and cabinets when preparing for dinner parties. As each task is completed, she gets great satisfaction from throwing the post-it away!

4. RIBBON

Ribbon is an essential aesthetic tool. Look for it on sale and at garage sales. Throw the ribbon you buy, along with all the bows and ribbons you get on gifts, plants, etc. into a basket or drawer, so that you have one place to go when you need it. Don't forget interesting twines and raffia.

LAZYQUICK TIPS
Roundabout Ribbon

PARTIES

Take wide wire-edged ribbon and run it down the center of the table, twisting it among small vases of flowers and clusters of candles. For children's parties, use lots of bright-colored curling ribbon, festively strewn about.

PILLOWS

You can tie (like a package) a beautiful satin or French ribbon over plain pillows to jazz them up.

WINDOW COVERINGS

Make a swag of material across the window like a valance and use ribbon to tie big bows on the corners where attached. Use hidden safety pins, if necessary.

PLANTS/CANDLESTICKS/FLOWER ARRANGEMENTS

Putting the right bow around just about anything can be the finishing touch or the perfect accent.

5. ZIPLOC BAGS

These bags are useful far beyond the kitchen door. They are the most multi-purpose, cross-gender, cross-age, cross-dressing item in your organizational arsenal. You'll want every size from the wee snacky size to the largest two-gallon bags.

THE MAGIC OF ZIPLOCS

TRAVELING BAGS

Use Ziplocs for traveling to protect your shampoos, etc. from leaking. Use them as a see-through way to organize and protect your passports/paperwork, jewelry, film and lingerie. You can take extra empty bags for your dirty clothes and shoes. Make a little Emergency Comfort Kit: tea, powdered lemonade, powdered cream, sugar, coffee, hot chocolate, etc. or an Emergency First Aid Kit with aspirin, Band-Aids, Neosporin, Q-tips, Handiwipes, etc.

AROUND THE HOUSE

Ziplocs can be used in just about every room. They are easy to use and simple to label. We suggest using Sharpie pens.

PAMPHLETS/INSTRUCTIONS/WARRANTIES: For appliances and tools in the house or garage.

continued...

GAME AND TOY PIECES: To your level of compulsion…you can label them as specifically as "Lego Dragon" or just throw all little pieces into a bag to be sorted by whomever cares (if someone does).

DESK: Use Ziplocs to keep greeting cards, stamps, and mailer labels from getting all mixed up in your drawers. In the end it will save you time and the contents will stay in good shape.

COSMETICS/MEDICINES: Organize the things that would normally fall to the bottom of a bathroom drawer – samples from the doctor, lipsticks, cotton balls, Q-tips, etc. If you want to keep a smaller amount of something handy, like safety pins, put a handful in a Ziploc in your drawer.

CHRISTMAS PARAPHERNALIA: Put extra Christmas light bulbs and fuses in small Ziplocs.

LOOSE PHOTOS: If you want to keep some photos separate from your main photo storage place, put them in a Ziploc.

KID'S ARTWORK/IMPORTANT FILING: When you want to protect art until you can frame it or put it in a proper book, put it in a large Ziploc. It's better than leaving it in a drawer alone where it can be harmed. Paperwork that needs to be filed can be put in bags for protection until properly filed.

6. SHARPIES

Black Sharpie brand permanent markers in fine and extra fine are essential Lazy Woman tools. They can be used for almost everything – kids' clothes, lunch boxes, CD's, cassettes, storage boxes. They last a very long time and keep their strong tip to the end.

7. INDUSTRIAL STRENGTH STAPLER/TACKER

These magnificent machines can attach fabric, wire mesh, plastic, canvas, upholstery, paper, cardboard – anything that needs to be hooked or re-hooked, attached or re-attached. They are strong and easy to use.

8. MUSEUM PUTTY

Museum Putty is a great way to secure lightweight objects from falling if you want a temporary bond. It comes off without leaving a trace if you need to remove it!

9. SUPER CUTTERS

There are many incarnations of the multi-purpose cutting tool in your local hardware store. This tool can save your life. It can prune roses, cut wire, cardboard, metal, plastic, etc.

10. POWER DRILL/SCREWDRIVER

Drill and screwdriver in one? What could be more efficient? Even if you've never used a power tool before, we recommend you try this one. The battery operated one is lightweight and powerful, but not dangerous.

Feathering the Lazy Woman's Nest

THE LAZY WOMAN'S FAMILY

Family

Parenting

Parents

Kids

Pregnancy

Empty Nest

Pets

INTRODUCTION

In an ideal world, we would live like fish in the sea, surrounded by nourishment, peaceful splendor, and thrive happily. In an ideal world, we would find this within our family.

Giving, receiving, yielding, celebrating, allowing space, taking time, needing, draining, expecting are all part of the balancing act in the ecosystem we call family. It's hard to keep it all working smoothly.

Now, where does the Lazy Woman fit into this delicate world? Like the mermaid beautifully moving from land to sea, she ebbs and flows, learning to balance her needs with those of her family. For some women, family needs are few. For others, a tsunami of family demands wipes out any hope of serenity.

What do you do when you are struggling to support an aging parent, nourish a marriage, raise children, help a sister through a divorce, and still need to have dinner on the table by 7 o'clock? How do you find time to take care of your needs? Where is your Hammock Time?

When you feel yourself floundering, remember to relax and float. When you are drowning, the more effort that you expend the faster you sink. Instead of fighting the tide, maybe this is the night to make scrambled eggs for dinner, tuck the kids in bed and be the Lazy Mermaid... take a long, sweetly scented bath.

FAMILY

The family – that dear octopus from whose tentacles we never quite escape, nor, in our inmost hearts, ever quite wish to.

– Dodie Smith, *Dear Octopus*

Family is one of those words – like sex, religion, money and love – that elicits a strong reaction from almost everyone. You praise or damn your family based on your experiences growing up. The media usually adds to these extremes with its pictures of either idealized or totally dysfunctional families. Most families, however, are some mix of oppressing and nurturing.

The Lazy Woman's Way is to keep intact the parts of the family that nourish and release those that don't. This can mean breaking the bonds of a toxic family, accepting the flaws of related but not always compatible family members, or creating a "family" where there is lasting love, respect, and support.

In the section on Holidays in Chapter 5 there are tips for managing exposure to a family setting that is problematic. Making peace within yourself is essential to a lazy life. Practice forgiveness no matter what has been done to you, but don't continue to allow yourself to be mistreated by family members.

Fortunately, the family is a changeable institution, subject to improvement. You can take what, if anything, works from your childhood and fashion your own ideal. There are excellent resources – books, classes, workshops – that offer insight and direction. (Check the Lazy Woman Resources in the back of the book for our favorites.) A sense of family is essential. Sometimes this is found with people with whom we share biology and history, and sometimes it's not.

Judie: *Nothing has shown me that families can be built more than adopting our son, Max. He is our son and we are his parents. Yes, he has biological parents and he might want to meet them someday. In some sense, they became part of our family when he did. And certainly his birth sister and her adoptive family are part of our family. We include them in our prayers, count them when we name his sisters, and travel to visit them as often as we can. With openness and commitment we have developed ties of relatedness without the ties of blood. Although I still get a little irritated when I hear people ask Max, "Is that your real mother?" or people say to me, "You seem to love him as much as your own children", I try to forgive their insensitivity and ignorance. As I tell Max, we are all here to teach each other lessons in life, clearly one of ours is to teach what it means to be a family.*

> " Every family is a "normal" family – no matter whether it has one parent, two or no children at all. A family can be made up of any combination of people, heterosexual or homosexual, who share their lives in an intimate (not necessarily sexual) way…Wherever there is lasting love, there is a family. "

– Shere Hite, *The Hite Report on the Family*

Whether you are fine tuning your definition of family, creating new rituals, healing relationship dynamics, or making some major changes in how you interact with your family, it is helpful to be light-hearted and enjoy whatever stage your family is in right now. Build for tomorrow but live in today.

PARENTING

Before I got married I had six theories about raising children; now I have six children, and no theories.

– Lord Rochester

Ordinarily, the words parenting and lazy would not be used in the same sentence. The very fact that it requires the care of another human being makes parenting a labor-intensive job. For the Lazy Woman, however, being able to parent with more enjoyment and less stress makes life a little lighter. Since there are as many opinions on parenting as there are people, it's not as easy as learning how to operate a computer or fly a jet plane. There is no instruction manual or big book in the sky that tells us just how to do it. This brings us to a major stumbling block for many parents.

THE OPINIONS OF OTHERS AND OTHER AGGRAVATING OUTSIDE INFLUENCES

It is especially difficult if the "others" include some form of shared custody: an ex-mate, relative caretaker or any other participating adult. Even when you agree on your approach, it's hard to feel confident during the bumpy times in a child's development. When there is someone criticizing and/or undermining your parenting, it can be overwhelming. There are things you can do to ease the tension.

1. LOOK HONESTLY AT THE ROLE YOU PLAY. Are you being too controlling? Many things that you think are mandatory can be made flexible without harming your child. If the other "parent" won't agree to set the same limits for behavior, dress, sleep, snacks, homework, etc. give up arguing with them about it. You're not going to change their mind and if it's a power struggle it will only reinforce their resistance to cooperating with you.

2. BE HONEST WITH YOUR CHILD. Let your children know that you both love them, but that grown-ups don't always agree on how to raise kids. Don't deny the tension. You don't have to go into details but let them know that there are different rules when they're with you.

3. DO NOT MAKE THE OTHER PERSON THE BAD GUY. As much as you may feel justified, this is one of the worst things you can do to your child. They have to spend time with that person. It's difficult enough for them to make transitions between households without the added burden of being caught between warring caregivers.

4. KNOW WHEN TO SEEK HELP. If you can get the other "parent" to participate, that's great. If your kids are old enough, include them. Just being in a room together with a facilitator asking questions can give everyone a chance to be heard. When you can't involve the other party and your child is too young, seek out support and

guidance for yourself. As with all stressful situations, using the Lazy Woman's Seven Commandments as mantras when you are stuck in fear, anger, anxiety, resentment, etc. can help you find an inner balance.

The tips above are helpful also when the conflict is within the same household. In situations where you don't agree with your mate about how to parent, the results can range from tense to explosive.

Judie: *Even after 35 years of marriage, Jay and I don't always have the same parenting style. We can be in agreement about a rule or a policy but there are times when one or the other of us feels rules can be broken and the other one doesn't. I have a really hard time when I come home late on a weeknight and Jay should have had Max long in bed, and I find them in front of the television. Jay may be asleep, but Max never is. I have to then deal with my irritation without becoming derailed, get Max into bed and then face the reality of getting him up the next morning – and he's not a morning person to begin with!*

I have talked with Max and Jay about this, but I've pretty much chosen to allow them to have the relationship that they have, knowing that some of this is about bonding. I've also, though, recognized my controlling ways and have backed off, letting them deal with the consequences. Jay needs to get Max up in the morning after they've chosen to stay up together and Max needs to learn how choosing to stay up late makes him feel the next day.

Try to achieve a compromise in your parenting styles and look for magazine articles, talks, or workshops on parenting at a local church, school or recreation center. There are hundreds of books on parenting. Many of them offer sound advice. We have included some of our favorites in the Lazy Woman Resources in the back of the book. Even a small amount of common ground on how to parent will diffuse the tension and your kids will witness the art of compromise, which is essential for a lazy life.

Remember that no one has an absolute lock on how to best raise a child. We are all beginners, making it up as we go along.

> **❝If** *only we could have them back as babies today, now that we have some idea what to do with them.* ❞
>
> – Nancy Mairs, *Ordinary Times*

LAZYQUICK TIPS

Avoiding the Pitfalls of Parenting

STAY IN THE PRESENT

Don't get stuck worrying about the future. Will I ever have a life again? Will Susie ever be potty-trained? How will I live through their teenage years? Being around kids with an eye to enjoying the moment can transform the experience. Remember that no one you know went off to high school in diapers and your parents survived your teen years!

TAKE TIME TO JUST "BE" WITH YOUR KIDS

If you get lost in parental responsibilities, having fun with your kids can get left out. It might take leaving the dishes in the sink, but make time to play a game or go to the park. Don't fill every drive to school or errands with lectures or cell phone conversations. Hang out with your kids and LISTEN to them.

CHOOSE YOUR BATTLES

Monitoring an endless list of do's and dont's takes time and energy. Is the price you pay for getting kids to keep their room clean worth it? The fewer restrictions, the more relaxed you and your child will be. Save the "nevers" for the big stuff.

continued...

Admit You Have Children

Parenting is easier in a child-friendly environment. Avoid a pristine museum-like environment and you'll eliminate the constant cry, "Don't touch that!"

Step Back

Let go of your picture of perfect parenting. When you think you have all the answers, there's no room to respond to your child's individual personality.

Think Outside the Box

When you are stuck in an ongoing battle, try a new approach. If you have trouble getting your child to eat well, fix an "ice-cream-like" vitamin-packed smoothie. Sneak finely chopped vegetables into pasta sauce or soup. If your child fights reading, try books on tape; it may break the cycle of resistance and negativity associated with reading.

ZERO TOLERANCE:
THE THINGS YOU ABSOLUTELY FORBID

Lazy Women need to limit the things for which they have zero tolerance. Just the term implies a lot of monitoring, so choose carefully. With your children, rules will change as they age. When they are small, there are the obvious dangers – playing with matches, running in the street, being in unsafe areas, etc. After that, parents set their own arbitrary guidelines about how high kids can climb, where they can play, what they can eat, and so on. As they get older the face of danger changes – sex, drugs, alcohol, violence. There is an urgency to cement good values before they leave home.

As children ready themselves to move out into the world, giving them more freedom allows them to practice making choices. Eventually, they will need to make all their own decisions. If they haven't had any *practice*, how will they manage the endless stream of decisions needed to live independently?

So, when composing a zero tolerance list, balance the need to protect your kids and to impart values while allowing them the opportunity to make their own choices.

IS IT REALLY YOUR BUSINESS?

As kids become teenagers, their dress, hair styles, music, etc. become their personal style, their *sense of self*. Sometimes these interests follow them into young adulthood, but most often it's a "phase." It can be scary, but some of this stuff is simply not your business and you have to honor that. Ask yourself: Is this dangerous? Is it illegal, destructive, or hurtful? It's natural when they push the envelope in search of independence. They can be rude, messy, and full of "leave me alone," but now, perhaps more than ever, your child needs to feel loved.

Understand that their gruffness or sharp criticisms are coming from insecurity and adolescent confusion and don't take it personally. Avoid getting locked in a power struggle. Keep the bridge of affection intact with hugs, pats, and shoulder rubs, and don't be hurt or give up when they pull away. Humor, a light touch, and another try will allow a growing child the space to accept love and affection. Remember, Lazy Woman's Commandment #7: You are a separate person.

PARENTS

For some people the mere mention of parents stirs warm memories and thoughts of loving relationships. For others it elicits feelings of anger, resentment, or fear. Between these extremes lie the endless individual responses to this most complex relationship. Your parents color the whole of your development, not just during your childhood. Their influence lives on within you, in how you perceive yourself and the world.

> "One reason you are stricken when your parents die is that the audience you've been aiming at all your life – shocking it, pleasing it – has suddenly left the theater."

– Katherine Whitehorn, *The Observer*

Even if you were adopted and never met your birth parents, they affect you. You wonder what they are like, look like, if they are still alive, what your life would have been like if....and the ultimate question – how they could have given you up if they loved you.

Making peace with your parents – birth, adoptive, foster, step, grand or whoever raised you – gives you somewhat of a clean slate about how you choose to live life. If you are always trying to please them, perform up to their expectations, defy them, or prove them wrong, you will live in reaction to your parents.

Recently, Judie's husband, Jay, went backpacking with two young men in their early thirties. Around the campfire they got into a vigorous debate about their fathers. One of them wished that his father had taken more time from his career to spend with his family. The other had a very active father who didn't always keep his job or pay the bills. They were both insistent that they would have been better off with the other's father. When they asked Jay his opinion, he told them that by the time he was in his forties he had grown to see that his parents had done the best they could with the tools they were given. He was grateful to have realized this several years before they died so that he could be thankful for what they had given him and forgive their errors.

LAZYQUICK TIPS

Making Peace with your Parents

FORGIVENESS

Work to achieve forgiveness. It may help to see a therapist or spiritual counselor. Do whatever it takes.

PUSHING OLD BUTTONS

Develop awareness of old emotional ties: sibling rivalry, being treated like a child, needing to rebel. These will probably always be there, but when you are aware of them you can change how you react.

LIMIT YOUR EXPOSURE

If the relationship causes you problems, limit your exposure. You choose when, where, and how you spend time with your parents, whether in person or on the phone.

LETTING GO

If they are truly abusive or toxic, sever contact without guilt, work on letting go of your anger, and embrace positive parental figures in your life.

CHAPTER FOUR

KIDS

Kids will be kids. What does that mean? Is it an excuse for bad behavior or a cry for more tolerance? Everyone who's *never* raised a child has an opinion on just how it should be done. Some of us who have parented several kids have had the gift of one who challenges all our parenting wisdom. For Judie, kids (her own and other people's) have always been central to her life. Bridget, who has never been sure she wanted kids of her own, has been happy with the "Aunt Bridget" role, spending limited time with her friends' kids.

If you are childless and kids are not your cup of tea, it's easiest to limit the time spent with them. Admit to yourself, your relatives, friends, and neighbors that you'd rather not spend a lot of time around kids: "Nothing personal, they're delightful," but you're just not a "kid person." Above all, do not get sucked into an "oh, but if you only spent more time with them" debate. Find other ways to acknowledge the kids in your social or family circle. Send cards or give gifts on appropriate occasions. Listen when their parents share likes and dislikes. Try to be open to a relationship when they hit an age or stage you can really enjoy.

If you already have children when you discover that you are "not a kid person," it's a bit trickier to manage. There are ways to make your time spent with kids more enjoyable, or at least, less stressful. (See Parenting for tips.)

Whether they are yours or other people's, children are our legacy and there is much to be gained by interacting with them. We all have something to give to kids and it is tremendously rewarding to contribute to a child's life.

Even if you don't want to interact directly with kids, you can help them through fundraising, collecting clothes or toys, and working behind the scenes for children's organizations.

Instead of feeling guilty that you aren't contributing anything (which is very un-lazy, by the way), try just one small gesture. Even with a minimal, once-yearly effort, you will make a contribution and feel connected to the future, which makes for a happier and more fulfilled life.

PREGNANCY

Nowadays, pregnancy is a possibility for more women than ever before. Scientifically and socially, there have never been more choices. One thing, however, is still true: once you have a child, your life will be changed forever. You will be a parent, which is, by its nature, not a lazy job.

SO YOU WANT TO GET PREGNANT?

There are an endless number of books written with advice on whether, why, why not, when, and even how to get pregnant. What they can't do is make the decision for you or guarantee the results. Once again we suggest adopting the Lazy Woman's attitude about trying to get pregnant. If you use Lazy Woman's Commandment # 2 and "Live in the moment," you can move to Lazy Woman's Commandment #3 and "Take pleasure in what you have." Try to be present in every moment, grateful for the every day treasures, knowing that your life rests in the hands of God. Not only does this make each day more fulfilling, but according to scientific research, it increases your chances of becoming pregnant. Infertility and tension often go hand in hand. As with everything you want in life, the harder you to try to control the outcome, the greater the struggle.

Both of us have friends who have dealt with trying to get pregnant. Three of them had actually started the adoption process and within weeks became pregnant. Of course, it's not always a matter of just releasing expectations or tensions. But no matter what your decisions are about how to achieve pregnancy, life will be more enjoyable if you take the focus off of getting pregnant.

PREGNANT: BLOOMING WITHIN YOUR SKIN

One of life's great ironies is that time spent anxiously awaiting pregnancy is often followed by time anxiously awaiting the birth. Once again, the Lazy Woman's Way is to live every moment, enjoy what you are given, and leave the worrying to God! This is the one and only time you will be in your third month of pregnancy with this child: the only time you will be in this place, in this state of being, so savor every moment. Sometimes it helps to stand outside yourself, like an observer. Notice your thoughts and emotions: "Oh, I'm worrying about the labor again" or "I feel fat and ugly" or "If I'm so exhausted now, how will I ever survive night feedings?" These are just your thoughts. If you let them come and go without latching on to them, without thinking that you actually have to do something about them, you can be present to experience your pregnancy, with all the wonder and awe appropriate to the miracle unfolding within you.

WHAT TO WEAR, WHAT TO WEAR?

Thank God for the age of great variety and good design in maternity clothes. You can go loose and baggy or stretchy and clingy – just as long as it's comfortable.

• Make sure your **shoes** provide good support, are comfy, and adapt to your ever-inflating feet!

• Don't rush into maternity **clothes** or you'll tire of them way before you deliver. Use big men's shirts and tees over your jeans for as long as you can. You can use a strong rubber band to extend unbuttoned "regular" waist-bands.

• Don't try to dress like someone else if it's not your **style**. You can see a pregnant celebrity in a magazine – exquisitely airbrushed – and be depressed when the same outfit makes you look and feel like a cow.

• Invest in good, supportive **bras** and change your bra-size as you progress through your pregnancy.

• Clothes **swap** with friends to increase your selection and stay simple: simple styles, solid colors.

OH NO! HOW DID THIS HAPPEN?

When you see the commercials on T.V. for home pregnancy tests the woman are all glowing with the results, plan a special dinner, and tell their equally excited husbands the glorious news. This is, of course, sometimes the scenario. But it probably is matched by the number of times the results are not so well received: the times when the woman is praying to be pregnant but isn't and sadly praying not to be but is.

An unwanted pregnancy is one of the most difficult situations a woman can face. It has a tremendous impact on her life, her immediate circle of family and friends, and on the larger circle of her society. The ramifications are personal, spiritual, societal, and increasingly political. In our section on *Sex* we urge woman to take responsibility for their sexuality. Own it, be comfortable with it, and above all protect it. The technology is here: use it. And if that doesn't make you safe enough, abstain from intercourse. There are hundreds of ways to have satisfying sex.

EMPTY NEST

"When mothers talk about the depression of the empty nest, they're not mourning the passing of all those wet towels on the floor, the music that numbs your teeth, or even the bottle of capless shampoo dribbling down the shower drain. They're upset because they've gone from supervisor of a child's life to a spectator. It's like being the vice president of the United States."

– Erma Bombeck

If you pay attention, this is something you can prepare for while the nest is still full. It's sometimes difficult to go from having children in the home to living without the daily acts of parenting. There are, though, things you can do to ease the transition. If you follow these tips, you can also improve the quality of your life even while the kids are still at home!

LAZYQUICK TIPS

Preparing for the Empty Nest

USE THE LAZY WOMAN'S SEVENTH COMMANDMENT

Remind yourself "You are a separate person." If you let go of the need to control the "outcomes" in your kids' lives, you will enjoy their years as children more, be ready to parent an adult, and have your own full life.

MAINTAIN OTHER RELATIONSHIPS

Remember to develop and maintain outside relationships. If you are married, be sure you don't lose the fun and intimacy with your partner. Make time to see friends – even if it's just to have a cup of tea, take a walk or talk on the phone. These will be your daily relationships after the kids are gone.

DEVELOP AND MAINTAIN PERSONAL INTERESTS

It's great to be involved in kid-related activities, but don't lose touch with your own interests – gardening, painting, tennis, etc. You will be more fulfilled, allow your child more space to grow, and be better prepared for life without kids in the house.

WHEN THE NEST "FEELS" EMPTY

Some moms start feeling the empty nest syndrome when the kids are all in school for full days. Bridget has a friend who started feeling like she might want another baby around that time. She also, though, at this time started to focus on herself more. She had always wanted to try drumming. She took a class and found that she was a natural drummer and in fact ended up playing in a band! Her husband and kids were delighted to see this newfound spark in her life, and she felt great excelling in something besides parenting. That empty nest feeling can just be a call to a different kind of creativity.

RETURN TO THE NEST

The rising trend is to have the birds return to the nest at some point. If you have looked forward to those empty nest years, this can present a difficult situation. You need to decide what works for you. If your space is small and your life has gone in a new direction, you may need to speak to your kids about how you can support them without having them actually live with you.

Judie: *My experience of the empty nest has been incomplete and sporadic. As soon as my children were off to college, we became foster parents to a relative's child and took in a series of young people (friends of our kids) that needed a temporary place to stay. When our kids would come home for a holiday or for the summer, we would juggle rooms and share space. Then our son, Max, came to us as a week-old baby. All of a sudden, we realized our fear of losing him was stronger than our concern about starting over as parents in our forties. So, full-time parenting exists simultaneously with the comings and goings of the adult kids, who have come and gone far more times than I can count. Whatever the transition, we have a big house and an open door. Sometimes it's chaotic and it's not always easy, but as with all parenting, it has its rewards. If you don't want your home to be without kids, I highly recommend foster children or adoption. Our "second family" has brought us great joy, new friends, and never a dull moment.*

Even if you are just in the nest building phase – it's good to use the Lazy Woman's Commandment #7, "You are a separate person." Remember *yourself* in the bigger picture that is your family.

PETS

"We're goldfish people, we're ant farm people, we're not dog people!"

– Beethoven, the movie

Are you a dog person, a cat person, a fish person? Maybe you love the freedom and serenity of having no animals in the house. Even if part of you would like to have a pet, often the laziest answer is not to have one at all. Like children, they take work and can bring a lot of joy, but they aren't for everyone.

Bridget: *I was thinking about getting a cat, my first pet as an adult. It took me months to make the decision. I had a very neurotic and bizarre worry: that I would never be completely alone in my house again. I didn't want to be responsible for any living thing 24 hours a day. The deciding factor was my friend, Ellie, who said, "A cat will make you laugh and laugh and laugh." I thought that had to be just about the best reason ever to get a cat. Ellie was right – I've had a lot of laughs. The joy has far outweighed the responsibilities.*

If you enjoy observing animals but you don't want any responsibility, put a bird feeder outside your window. That way, you get to watch birds (and squirrels!) without having to use a pooper-scooper or empty a litter box!

Any animal – even a fish or bird – needs care and attention. If you don't have the time that they need, then don't get them (or don't let your child talk you into one). If your child wants a pet, make sure that they are old enough to take care of it themselves – but even then *you* will have to monitor their care.

Even with the annoyances there's a lot of joy and love that come from the relationship you have with an animal. The Lazy Woman gets to appreciate her animals and receive a lot of love, while keeping the drudgery of their maintenance to a minimum.

LAZYQUICK TIPS
Pets 101

DOG TRAINING: The laziest way to deal with a dog in the long run is to get it trained in short order. Even if you hire someone else to do it for you, you still have to reinforce it.

LITTER BOX TRAINING: Most cats have a natural instinct to use the litter box. It can help to isolate them with it in a bathroom they've got it down. Even then, you still may have to deal with spraying and/or "pissed off" cats. See "Carpet Boo Boos".

VETERINARIANS: A Lazy Woman's Vet will: 1) give you phone advice, 2) see your pet at the last minute, 3) reasonably charge you, and 4) give quality care. Personal recommendations are the best way to find one.

WALKING: Neither you nor your dog is in danger of being OVER-walked! So, here is one of those double-benefit activities. Let the guilt over your pent-up pet help push you out the door.

FEEDING: Feeding leftovers to your pets sounds lazy, but sometimes leads to health problems or allergies which result in the need for special shampoos, trips to the vet, allergy shots, salves or pills.

LAZYQUICK TIPS
When "Pepé le Pieux" Comes to Call

CARPET BOO BOOS

Nature's Miracle, any similar pet odor/stain remover, or white vinegar all work. Put paper towels or rags on the puddle and step on it to sop up the urine or pick up the poop. Then pour the solution onto the spot and sop it up with towels or rags. Repeat a couple of times.

SKUNK SMELL

Tomato juice or any tomato-based product works because of the acid in the tomatoes. Pour it on the animal and rub it into their fur. After you rinse off the juice, shampoo with a scented shampoo. If you have aromatherapy oils, throw a few drops on while shampooing. Or, for a truly lazy solution, take them to the groomer in the morning.

EAR CLEANING

For smelly ears, try this home remedy. Mix 1/2 cup of witch hazel, 1/4 cup of vinegar and 1/4 cup of water. Drop a teaspoon or so into the ear, rub the outside of the ear. If it continues to be a problem, take them to the vet for treatment because ear infections can lead to hearing loss.

The Crazy World We Live In

THE LAZY WOMAN'S VIEW

Juggling

Technology

Money

Time

Travel

Work

To Do (Be Do Be Do)

Shopping

Gifts

Holidays

INTRODUCTION

Many airports have automatic walkways. Most people find them a relief at one time or another. Some travelers prefer their own leg power no matter how much luggage they have. There are many choices as we go through the various "airports" of our lives. We have to decide every day when we want to take the faster, high-tech road or the slower, simpler route.

Information technology is developing more rapidly than even the stock market can keep up with. As you read this, the future ramifications of human genome research are as unfathomable as sending a man to the moon was 100 years ago. Every day we synchronize our watches to this ever-accelerating pace. Everywhere we turn, there are experts touting new improved methods of saving time and we gravitate toward them, just as we gravitate toward the automatic walkway.

We assume that our lives will improve if we get things done more quickly and efficiently. Then we start to expect hot food in seconds, computers that boot up instantly, immediate responses via email, fax, cellphone and page. Is it ever fast enough or advanced enough? We covet each new level of advancement.

Can we stay on the automatic walkway and yet create a lazy attitude? When is there time for peace and tranquility? We need to be able to get on and off the walkway. Sometimes we need to walk at a slower pace, to exercise our legs, lungs, and heart, and savor the moment. You can *choose* to be conscious of when you let the walkway take you and when you step off.

JUGGLING

The pace of life today (unless you live in a monastery!) demands that women be able to juggle a vast array of tasks and responsibilities. We are supposed to exercise, be attractive, work, cook, care for families (if we have them), entertain, keep a beautiful home, maintain our friendships, and have time for relaxation and fun!

We're always juggling. Do I plant the flowers I just bought or finish cleaning the kitchen? Do I go to the movie I've been dying to see or do I work late? Should I exercise now, or pay bills? This is the everyday scenario – deciding how to fit it all in, balancing your needs and the needs of your family, friends, employer, financial obligations, health, etc.

The only time juggling is a worrisome issue is when you notice the balls are dropping: food is rotting in the fridge, the plants are dying before you even get them in the ground, and your family is complaining that *all* the clothes are dirty.

There is an element of ego in all choices. You need to take a look at what ego payoff is connected with the things you do. *Am I flattered when someone asks me to participate? Does this just make me look better, feel more successful, or does it contribute to the quality of my life?* These are the questions you need to ask yourself when choosing which balls to keep in the air, and which to simply let roll away. (See Choices in Chapter 7.)

LAZYQUICK TIPS
Juggling

STOP AND TAKE STOCK!

When you find yourself distressed by balls bouncing at your feet, you need to STOP and TAKE STOCK. Some things you know you can't let drop, but much of what we feel we have to do is actually expendable, or at least alterable. Some tasks are meant to be dropped.

BACK BURNER

Sometimes you need to use the back burner and put something on it indefinitely. Adding to your garden, painting the bedroom or taking up tennis may have to wait. Put it on the infamous "To Do" List.

EDIT

Say NO to all non-essential requests. It's easier to turn someone down when they ask a favor or want you to join a committee than it is after you say "Yes" and struggle to meet the obligation.

JUGGLING BAG

Keep a large carry-all bag at the ready, by your front door or in your car with mail you need to sort, half-written letters, bills that need paying, something you've been trying to read, etc., so that when you have some "found time" you can take advantage of it.

TECHNOLOGY

Judie doesn't even like to read this word, let alone write about it or deal with it. She, a true Lazy Woman, wants technology to work for her, not to have to work for it. If you aren't willing to learn how to use it, it's just going to become a source of frustration. The Lazy Woman's Way to deal with Technology is:

- Ask **questions** *before* you buy.

- Arrange for good **tech support** (i.e. a person you can call or equipment that comes with tech support). This could be someone you know, someone in your family, or a neighbor. If you're reluctant to ask for their support, try a trade.

- Tape or write (with a Sharpie) the **800 number** on the equipment.

- Keep **manuals** *taped* to the equipment, stored underneath, or have one central location where all your manuals are kept, so there is no time wasted when you have a problem.

- Keep **supplies** handy. There's nothing worse than running out of ink in the middle of a print job or fax. Keep extra ink, batteries, paper, power cords, etc. in a central location for all your equipment.

- Keep things in good **repair**. Try to do the minimal maintenance before you have a problem. If you aren't a "techie," it's good to invest in the service contract that gets you in-home service.

QUESTIONS TO ASK BEFORE INVESTING IN NEW EQUIPMENT

• Is this going to be easy enough for me to use? How much training will it take?

• Will it really save me time and effort?

• To own is to maintain. Do I want to deal with having it repaired, buying ink, paper, tapes, batteries, etc.? What do I do if it does need to be repaired? Will I be lost when it's at the repair shop? Does the warranty give me a loaner? What's my back-up if it breaks down?

• Do I have room for it? Is it worth the space it's going to take up?

• Do I need it now or do I want to wait for the newer, faster, cheaper, smaller version soon to be on the market? You'll only have the latest model for a short time anyway, so just make sure it meets your economic and practical needs.

COMPUTERS

If you are not a computer user, your life will not become easier just by owning one. There is a learning curve, which implies at least some investment of time and energy. But, once you learn how to use it, a computer can be a great time-saving tool. You can do things at home any time of the day or night that would normally take a trip to a printer or the effort to go to a copy center.

If you think you are ready to enter the land of computers, spend some time trying out different kinds at a friend's house or a store.

Judie just bought her mom (who is 81) a no-brainer iMAC so that she could use it immediately, explore the Internet, or e-mail her friends without investing much time and energy. We're not here to advertise for Macintosh, but its paint-by numbers set-up can't be beat for computer novices. Be honest about how much time you can invest in learning a piece of equipment. Otherwise, it's a waste of money.

E-MAIL

Bridget, who spends a lot of time on a computer, relies on e-mail to make her life less complicated. She finds it to be a wonderful way to get silly, unimportant info off her desk. If she is already on-line, it's faster than picking up the phone. Also, she loves the new digital cameras that can send photos via e-mail within seconds.

Judie, who does not spend much time on a computer, doesn't use e-mail because it would be one more machine that had to be turned on and accessed to retrieve messages. She finds the voice mail on her phone to be enough of a communication venue in her life.

When Judie's friend, urging her to get e-mail, said, "You've got to get e-mail. It would make your life so much easier," Judie responded, "No, it wouldn't, it would make *your* life easier." The friend had to admit this was true. You have to make a decision about what works for you. Something that someone else couldn't live without is not necessarily going to be a time saver for you.

INTERNET

If you tend to be on your computer anyway, it can be a great resource. Some people find it addictive, because it is another world that can seductively lead you on an endless exploration. If you use the Internet, make sure you are enjoying yourself and no other part of your life is suffering.

Marriages and families have been adversely affected by the amount of time one person spends on the Internet. You need to pay attention to the time it takes you away from your loved ones.

FAX MACHINES

We love them. Most of them are easy to use and also provide a method of copying. It's a great gift to give parents or grandparents who live some distance away, as an instantaneous alternative to mail or email. Your toddler can fax a drawing to grandma or grandpa. It's an immediate connection to family and friends. You don't have to address an envelope, have a stamp, or even put it in the mailbox. It's handled and off your desk within moments.

TELEPHONES, ANSWERING MACHINES, CALLER ID, VOICE MAIL, CALL FORWARDING, ETC.

The telephone realm has become a world unto itself. Where are we going with this? Do you expect to be able to reach people or to need them to reach you at will? Do you want to be a slave to your phone? It's not lazy to feel you have to answer every call as soon as you get it. Keep it simple and make it work for you. Do you really have to hit *69 to call back the person that just hung up or watch your Caller ID box like a hawk? Think about it. Use whatever phone answering service you have to get some uninterrupted time for yourself or with your family. Do what works for you.

CELLPHONES/PAGERS/WALKIE-TALKIES

Be selective about giving out your cellphone/pager number (even if it has voice mail) because it is yet another thing that will keep you tied to someone else's agenda. Use your cellphone/pager as a tool for yourself, to make *your* life easier, not theirs. Remember: you can always turn it off!

The new generation of walkie-talkies have huge ranges. They're great because you only communicate with the people you choose. They come in handy if you are caravaning or are at a big event where you want to keep track of each other.

KITCHEN APPLIANCES

Some small appliances can catapult you into a new level of lazy! For instance, neither of us would ever be found in the kitchen up to our elbows in bread dough. Nor would we be found churning ice cream by hand. This is not to denigrate those of you who appreciate such endeavors. But if you are looking for the taste of home-made bread or ice cream, consider some of the great electric options. (See Cooking in Chapter 1.)

Some kitchen appliances can be more trouble than they are worth. They take longer to clean than to use. Others do things that you don't even need or want to do. If you don't use it, lose it so that you don't have to store it or feel pressured to use its expensive features.

MONEY

Most people have money issues – they have a lot or not enough, they feel they deserve more or are guilty about what they have; they think someone else has the money they deserve, or they hoard or overspend it. Is money the root of all evil or would it be the answer to all your prayers? Money is not a neutral subject for anyone.

If your relationship with money is off, it takes a toll on daily living. You have to earn it and spend it over and over again. Unless you are extremely wealthy, you have to monitor your spending to some extent.

There are people who expose their deepest flaws in relationship to money. For instance, we all have Grinch-like characters in our lives. Maybe they don't hoard money; maybe they just refuse to buy gifts. Bridget had a relative who was even more extreme than the Grinch. He insisted that people use only four squares of toilet paper in his home (no one did, of course, but they played along.) In his later years, he got even crazier and licked his plates clean so that he could avoid using water. This man died with millions in the bank. Certainly no one reading this book is this extreme in their behavior, but the example illustrates how out of control people can be around money.

To the best of their ability, Lazy Women want to make peace with money. That way, the lack of it, guilt over it or desire for more, won't permeate their lives. We all have times of more or less ease with money. Sometimes, it's related to how much we actually have, sometimes it's related to how much we're spending, and sometimes it's related to denial about our financial situation. If you have serious spending problems, you may find Debtors Anonymous (an offshoot of the Alcoholics Anonymous Program) helpful. Also, consult Lazy Woman Resources. Life is enough work without having to dig yourself out of debt. There is nothing lazy about constantly struggling with financial woes.

Most of us can at least fine-tune our financial attitudes and behavior. If you need a course of action, there are books and seminars that are especially accessible to women today. If you share this concern with a friend, make a pact to support each other to find a money management plan. Enrolling in a class or seeking counsel together can be less daunting, particularly when dealing with such big issues.

> **"***Never ask of money spent
> Where the spender thinks it went.
> Nobody was ever meant
> To remember or invent
> What he did with every cent.***"**
>
> – Robert Frost

Now, for the dreaded "B" word: Budget. Just the sound of it strikes terror in your heart. Banish the BUDGET from the Lazy Woman's Kingdom! We will *manage* our money with spirit and sanity and not be "put" on a budget like Lucy Ricardo!

LAZY WOMEN DON'T "BUDGET" THEIR MONEY, THEY MANAGE IT!

WARNING: This could be painful…but, we promise, it's worthwhile and in the end, it's the Lazy Woman's Way to deal with money…maybe grab a cup of tea or a tiny bowl of Cheetos before you continue…

1. How much money
do you take home each month? .... _____

2. Be honest: What are your
bottom line expenses? .... _____

3. Be even more honest: What do you
actually end up spending? This is where
the almighty credit cards come into play,
taking you into a realm beyond your
paycheck, digging your way into a very
un-lazy situation: debt .... _____

If line 3 is *more* than line 1, go to "Getting Out of Credit Card Debt The Lazy Way."

If line 3 is *less* than line 1, then you are ready to start investing (if you haven't already). Go to the box on "Lazy Investments" on page 137.

Are we having fun yet?…

GETTING OUT OF CREDIT CARD DEBT THE LAZY WAY

GINSU KNIVES

If you can't cut down your use of credit cards, destroy them. Seriously, cut them up. Psyche yourself up for it. Know that in the long run you will have more money and a greater sense of power. You will never be at their mercy again. Get amped up and destroy them. You may regret it a minute after you do it – or at least the next time you reach for one – but it is the first step to getting your spending under control.

GO HOLLYWOOD

Write a script. Create any kind of mental scenario necessary to live without your credit cards. Trick yourself with thoughts of self-sacrifice, spiritual superiority, dramatic martyrdom. Pretend you are doing this for the betterment of mankind, for your children's future, putting your dog through college – whatever it takes to motivate you. Shift the fantasy to suit your needs. It actually gets easier once you get out of the credit card habit. The phrase, "I don't use credit cards anymore" will flow from your lips. You won't be jumping to cover the restaurant bill or to buy an extra gift for someone, but you will be more sane. Your friends will be in awe of you.

continued...

DEBT CONSOLIDATION

This is what you need if you are in really bad shape and for some people it is the laziest approach. A service will help you get all your bills together, negotiate monthly payments to each creditor and then bill you one amount each month, which will slowly whittle away your debt. You pay for these services, but it's worth it if you are overwhelmed by the thought of negotiating directly with creditors.

RECHARGE YOUR BATTERIES

During the time that you are paying off your credit cards without using them, you may feel sorry for yourself. So make sure you give yourself some TLC, especially around bill-paying time. Set aside an amount ($5, $20, or whatever you can afford) that you can use each month to buy something you've had to cut out or cut back on.

CREATE A DREAM LIST

Write down the things that you want to do or have in your life. Spend some time thinking about what it would take to make those dreams come true. How could having some expendable income get you closer to realizing your dreams? Keep your list handy so you can review it often and keep your dreams alive.

LAZY INVESTMENTS

401K Plans at Work. Always do what it takes to get the matching funds from your employer. It's like free money and it's the laziest way to make a buck.

Brokers. You choose the risk level you are comfortable with, and then let the broker do the rest. Find a broker you trust or that has been recommended to you.

Investment Clubs. You can join one that is already formed or get people together yourself. Sharing wisdom, past experiences and information are lazy ways to boost your investment know-how and get a little social time too.

BECOMING A LAZY FRU GAL

Being miserly is a drag and full of self-pity. But, if you come to the idea of being a Fru Gal with a goal that is going to make you feel better, it can be a fun thing to do. We call ourselves Lazy Fru Gals when we have a mission to accomplish – a fun vacation, a down payment to make, a credit card to pay off.

Our enthusiasm can even persuade other family members to skip a dinner out or forego a new stereo to share in the reward that the savings will bring. You can use a dry erase board to monitor the countdown to your goal: "Only $350 more to HAWAII!"

THE FRU GAL'S LAZY WAYS TO PICK UP EXTRA BUCKS

Coffee/Tea: Make coffee/tea at home instead of picking it up on the way to work.

Magazine Moratorium: They are expensive and usually useless after they've been read. Read them in the checkout line, at the doctor's office, or share a subscription with a friend.

Vending Machines/Liquor Stores: You can get a 6-pack of soda for about $1.50 at the market. Why spend six times as much?

Eliminate One Restaurant Meal a Week: Even the cheapie to-go meals add up.

Smokes and Cocktails: Set an amount by which you will reduce your intake. Stick with it. It's for a good cause – two good causes – your body and your wallet!

Public Library/Book Trade: You don't have to buy every darn book you want to read. Is it a book that you really need to own? Will you refer to it after you've read it? We often forget that the library exists after we've left school. You can also trade good reads with a friend or acquaintance who has your taste in books. If you can pick up just $5 a day each work week, you will save $25 a week, $100 a month...or $1200 a year! That's one heckuva bonus!

> *"I can't take it with me, I know*
> *But will it last until I go?"*

– Martha Newmeyer

The ultimate fear: running out of money before you run out of time. This is why, for practical purposes, getting out of debt and investing money makes sense. Unless you have a rich relative or win the lottery, having some retirement plan is essential in order to sleep well at night. You probably know the numbers, but the earlier you start the more you will have in the end. But it's never too late to start. If you invest just $100 each month starting at age 30, you will have invested $42,000 by the time you are 65 and it will yield you several hundred thousand if you have even a fairly good rate of return.

It doesn't do you any good to worry about the money you haven't saved in the past or fret about the future. Judie has already lost several friends her age who had, of course, expected to need a retirement plan. Any worrying they did was for naught. The important thing is that you start now to take some responsibility for the future, and then let it go. If necessary, consult an expert to jump-start the process. Getting started is the hardest part, but once you have your plan, it will be automatic and pretty darned lazy.

TIME

> *"Not losing time has been my permanent*
> *concern since I was three years old, when*
> *it dawned on me that time is the warp of*
> *life, its very fabric, something that you cannot*
> *buy, trade, steal, falsify or obtain by begging."*

– Nina Berberova

Time is huge. We all complain of never having enough of it. We see it as a commodity. Hence the phrases, "That would buy me some time," and "Time is money." We would all like to have more than 24 hours in a day, or just one more day a week, to get a head start on the rest of the world. Time always flies by too quickly, we say, particularly as we grow older. It's as if it's slipping through our fingers as we race to catch it.

TIME MACHINE: MAKING MORE TIME

How do you either make more time, or make yourself feel like you have more time? Look at your schedule. How much is self-imposed? What are the basic items on your agenda. Are you driven by these items? There are some things on your schedule that you can *un*choose. Be aware of how these arbitrary, self-imposed lists serve you. When they start to drive you to the point that you're stressed, with not enough time, you need to take control of your agenda instead of having your agenda take control of you.

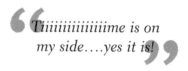

Tiiiiiiiiiiiiiime is on my side....yes it is!

– Mick Jagger

Part of the physics of creating time is how you *perceive* what you do with your time. For instance, some people spend a lot of time *judging* how their time is spent. They view keeping to a schedule as well-spent time, and deviating from it – getting caught in a book, talking to a friend too long, spending too much time in the hammock – as negative. They see it as a waste of time–when judging is the real waste of time.

THE LAZY WOMAN'S NEMESIS: TOTAL TIME WASTERS

We suggest that more than 5 minutes spent on any of the following is a total and utter waste but if any of these activities feed your soul, they are *not* a waste of time. Time is an entirely personal issue. This list gives you an idea of how to look for your own time wasters.

DARNING SOCKS: Socks are relatively cheap and walking on bunches of darned yarn is uncomfortable. Need we say more?

SUPERFLUOUS CLEANING: If you keep your house too clean, you're wasting time. No one needs to eat off your floor. Keep your plates clean, but let your floor gather a little dust before you clean it.

SUPERFLUOUS IRONING: Unless you love ironing, buy wrinkle-free fabrics or use a laundry service.

continued...

JUDGING/WORRYING/SELF-PITY/BLAME: Any negative emotional state that takes you out of the present and catapults you either to the past or future – as these all do – can become a chronic time waster. Some of us are addicted to one or all. If you are, try to stick to the 5 minute limit.

SHOULD'VE/COULD'VE/WOULD'VE AND OTHER POST-MORTEMS: Like the above, these mental acrobatics will not change the past or the future. We just believe that we can figure it all out if we think long and hard enough. But what really happens is that it brings back old emotions that have nothing to do with the present. You feel guilty, embarrassed, or angry all over again! Wasn't it bad enough the first time?

An added benefit to not spending your time stuck in analyzing the past or worrying about the future is that you are able to actually experience the present. When your husband is telling you about his day, you are really listening. When you're playing a board game with your child, you actually know when it's your turn. You are present, instead of stuck in your head – where, by the way, you will never experience the moment.

Living in the present is where happiness and contentment lie. Everything can *only* be experienced in the present. Getting to the place where you can live in the moment is not going to happen overnight, of course. It is an art that develops with practice, but it's well worth the effort and is the ultimate Lazy Woman's Way to live.

❝ *I've been on a calendar, but never on time.* ❞

– Marilyn Monroe

Do you synchronize your watch with the rest of society? Have you decided that being "on time" is a priority? You don't, of course, decide this once and then become *forever* on time. You decide on a daily or hourly basis, as to whether something is important to you. At some point, you will probably notice that either you tend to be on time or not. If people always comment on your lateness, then it's probably a pattern for you. Being late all the time may seem laid back, but it can make for a frantic life.

TIME ON YOUR BACK

Maybe the pressure of always having to be on time is making your life difficult. If being on time drives your life, then you might want to loosen up. On the other hand, do you get irritated when others aren't on time?

Either way, having a fixed time clock run your life means that your sense of time will always be that *there isn't enough*. With time, as with all of life, the ease is generally found in being flexible.

LAZYQUICK TIPS
Beat the Clock

READ THE MAGAZINES IN THE CHECKOUT LINE: It keeps you from getting agitated and you get a little reading in.

CLUSTER APPOINTMENTS: Schedule appointments back to back, so that you save time by not having to go out repeatedly.

READ YOUR MAIL WHILE WAITING: Whether it's the car wash, waiting for your kid to get out of school or at the dentist, you have waiting time to fill. If you carry your mail in a special folder or bag, you can read it, sort it, and sometimes even trash some of it before you get it into the house. Double points: less clutter, more time.

PUT YOUR SUPPLIES & TOOLS WHERE YOU USE THEM: Running around looking for things is a pain. It may take having more than one stapler, scissors, hammer, or screwdriver (see Organization in Chapter 3), but it will save you time and aggravation.

LET YOUR MACHINE/VOICE MAIL ANSWER THE PHONE: When you really need to pick up time, let the phone calls go unanswered for a while. Sometimes you actually have to turn the ringer off, so that you aren't tempted to answer.

CHAPTER FIVE

TRAVEL

*"To awaken quite alone in a strange town is one
of the most pleasant sensations in the world.
You are surrounded by adventure. You have
no idea what is in store for you, but you will,
if you are wise and know the art of travel,
let yourself go on the stream of the
unknown and accept whatever comes in
the spirit in which the gods may offer it."*

– Freya Stark, *Baghdad Sketches*, 1929

Travel is about perspective. When you go somewhere
new you get to experience different sights, sounds, textures, smells, and tastes. The mere fact that it is different
from what you are used to is wonderful. You also have the
opportunity to bring home pieces of what you have experienced, from new cooking techniques to unique daily rituals.

Bridget was traveling in Sri Lanka once with friends and
visited a Save the Children village. The children were
intrigued by the group of Americans and followed them on
their tour. At one point Bridget picked up a piece of yarn
from the ground and tied it around one of the little girl's
wrists. The girl was ecstatic that she had a bracelet! All
the kids then began bringing little pieces of thread and
yarn to have more bracelets made. From that experience,
Bridget learned a profound lesson about one person's
trash being another's treasure. Yes, it could have been
learned in downtown Los Angeles, but the children's perspective may not have been quite as exhilarating. It was

the coming together of two very different cultures that made a magical moment.

If you've been reluctant to travel, but always longed to, find a way to make it happen. Whether it's a quick weekend getaway, or the trip you've always dreamed of, start somewhere. Much will be dictated by your time, responsibilities, and budget. Whatever you do and however you do it, with a lazy attitude even the preparation can be fun.

With all the travel resources that are available, you don't have to be an expert to plan a good trip. If you're intimidated and need a person to work with, ask friends or co-workers to recommend travel agents. But if you like to spend time online, the Internet is an amazing source for making travel plans. You can search for good ticket prices and research hotels, restaurants, activities, and travel tips. In essence, you can create your own travel book by printing out the places you plan to stay, maps, and sites to see. Check out travelocity.com, expedia.com, travel.com, priceline.com, or just type in your destination and follow the links until you get what you need.

LAZYQUICK TIPS

Getting on the Road, in the Air, on the Trail

SAFETY: Educate yourself on the potential safety issues of your destination. Don't ignore the recommendations of the "experts" about which parts of town you should avoid, especially at night.

VALUABLES: In some places it's safe to leave valuables in your hotel room or hotel safe, but in others it's not. Generally, though, it's a good idea to keep them close to your body. You can buy very inexpensive, comfortable travel belts that can be hidden under clothes. Beware of using backpacks, which are vulnerable because they are out of your sight, so someone can touch them without your knowing it.

PACKING: What to take? This is not the time to be a walking fashion show, so build your clothing options around a couple of your favorite colors. This cuts down on overpacking and everything you bring goes together. Throw in a couple of scarves and belts as accents. This also allows you to layer your clothing to deal with climate changes. Shoes are the most important thing you pack because blistered, aching feet can ruin a trip. Make sure you start with comfortable walking shoes when you plan a wardrobe.

continued...

PACKING – ROLL, ROLL, ROLL YOUR CLOTHES: As strange as it may sound, you can pack more and it will be less wrinkled, if you roll it. Some people put a sheet of tissue paper over the article before they roll it. We, of course, are too lazy for that, and don't think it makes much of a difference. Smooth each garment and roll it up. You'll be surprised how easily all the rolls fit together and how much less space they take up than folded things!

PACKING: Ah, yet another use for the Ziploc. Put medicine, vitamins, cosmetics and toiletries in them. Use them even within your cosmetic bag, just in case something leaks. You can make a little Comfort Kit in a Ziploc with tea bags, instant coffee, hot cider, instant soup etc., so that just by adding hot water you can have a nice little "feel good" drink when there is no room service. Make a mini first aid kit with Bandaids, Neosporin, aspirin, Handi-Wipes and so on. Take empty Ziplocs for purchases, transporting wet clothes, or emergencies. Also take a few plastic grocery bags for dirty shoes or clothes.

WATER: Drink lots of water to battle the effects of jet lag. Bring bottled water with you, buy water as soon as you arrive and keep drinking it. It's easy to forget to drink water when you are distracted by your travels. Digestion is one thing that is often affected by travel, and water will help it.

CHAPTER FIVE

WORK

" I came to the conclusion that I hate work.
Turns out, I need to work. "

– Howard Stern, radio shock jock

The Lazy Woman realizes that work, whether inside or outside the home, is part of life; that we don't do our work perfectly all the time, and that work isn't all there is. When you notice that your work is eating your life – even when you aren't doing it, you're thinking about it – it's time to step back and find out how work can be a part of your life and not dominate it. We need to be able to see the way work shapes our daily lives and see it as our ally, not our enemy. It's important to look honestly at how our work meets our needs (financial, emotional, creative, intellectual), and assess whether we need to make a job change or an attitude shift.

If you hate your job, but you can't change jobs immediately, the Lazy Woman's Way is to enjoy each day until you can make a change. Do the job acting "as if" you like it. This will shift your daily experiences and with a open and positive attitude you can move towards the changes you want to make. (See As If in Chapter 8.)

CHANGE PARTNERS AND DANCE

People are reluctant to change their jobs. They stay in jobs they hate, because the known is more comfortable than the unknown. But sometimes changing jobs can bring amazing, unexpected gifts.

> *"Find a job you like and you add*
> *five days to every week."*

— H. Jackson Browne

Judie knows of a woman who, at 42, changed her entire life. She quit a job that she had come to hate, and went to beauty school. She became a colorist and loved her new life, the salon ambiance, and all that her new job brought to her. She had to step back and see clearly that her life as it was was not making her happy. It can be scary to leave the security of what you know, so it helps to enlist the support of family and friends. If you've always dreamed, or you have the recurring pull toward a certain job or career, as Joseph Campbell said, "Follow your bliss."

HOW TO MAKE YOUR TIME AT WORK
LESS EMOTIONALLY DRAINING

Whether we love or hate our jobs, there are ways that we allow ourselves to be emotionally drained by work. This leaves us with nothing left for our families or ourselves. The first step is to become aware of the people and situations that drain us.

DRAINING PEOPLE

VAMPIRE PEOPLE: They suck your energy with personal problems, neediness, constant criticism of you or others, and incessant chattering. You come away feeling like you need a blood transfusion.

TOWN CRIER: People who gossip make a career of knowing and disseminating information about other people. Gossip is impossible to avoid altogether, but professional gossips drain you and make you feel guilty.

THE ENFORCER: They know how everyone should do their job and they tell everyone - over and over. Whether they are in a position of authority or not, they are exhausting because you feel edgy and defensive when they are around.

DRAINING SITUATIONS

POWER STRUGGLES: Whether it's with an equal, a subordinate or someone above you, power struggles are tiring.

PERSONALITY CONFLICTS: There's always someone that just gets on your nerves and drives you crazy.

OVER-CRITICIZED AND UNDER-APPRECIATED: You know it if you feel it, whether warranted or not, and it's hard to tolerate.

TAKING ON THE BURDEN OF YOUR EMPLOYER'S WOES: Whether professional or personal, sometimes bosses turn to employees for relief from their own stresses.

LAZYQUICK TIPS
Dealing with the "Drainers"

IDENTIFY THE DRAIN

You may be drawn to certain positive aspects of the person, so it may take time to see clearly that they are having a negative impact on you. Pay attention to how you feel physically and emotionally when you are with them and/or after they leave. (See Friendship in Chapter 2.)

GRADUALLY BEGIN TO DISENGAGE

Be busy when the Drainer comes by, take a phone call, or remove yourself from the eye of the hurricane. You don't want to waste time and energy trying to be honest about your issues. They won't get it if you confront them. It's not like with family or friends, when working through an issue is worth it. You need to minimize your exposure. When you do get trapped, take it lightly. Don't give back opinions or responses. That's how they hook you. Change the subject: bore them with your new roof or your dog's dietary needs.

- CHANGE YOUR SCHEDULE: Avoid contact at lunch, breaks, after work.

- FIND ALLIES WHO GIVE ENERGY RATHER THAN TAKE IT: Again, how do you feel? Find people that make you feel energized.

LAZY WAYS TO
PRIORITIZE YOUR WORK
OR AVOID IT ALTOGETHER

Among the most fallacious of **myths** is: "A job worth doing is a job worth doing well." Not every job must be done well. Some jobs are meant to be done as quickly and easily as possible. Others are not meant to be done at all. For instance:

Cleaning your house before a party. It makes no sense to do in depth cleaning. Surface cleaning, good lighting and things that attract the senses (fragrant flowers, beautiful food, candles, etc.) are what people will notice, not your spotless floors or clean shelves.

Ironing anything that isn't seen. This includes sheets and underwear. If you can't see it, must it be perfect?

Cleaning before your cleaning service comes. Put away any important papers or objects and let the rest go!

Going above and beyond the call of duty. Choosing to do an even better job at a task that you are told to just "get done" is a waste. Save your high level work for the times when it is truly needed. Rewriting and revising an interoffice memo is ridiculous. Save energy for an important letter to a client – for something that actually moves you forward.

Above all, try to keep your work in perspective. All work is transitory. Urgent priorities today will be ancient history in a month. There are new priorities to come.

TO DO (BE DO BE DO)

To Do lists sound like a lot of work to some, but they can actually lighten your load – particularly when you are feeling overwhelmed. The best part of a To Do list is crossing out the tasks you've completed. Sometimes Bridget even puts things on her list that she has already completed, so she can get "credit" when she crosses them out!

If you need to live by a To Do list – even if it's just for a particularly busy time – have 1 or 2 places to keep it (i.e. purse, desk, bulletin board, refrigerator). If you lose the list, don't panic. Take a deep breath and you will probably start to remember what you wrote down. Keep in mind, this isn't the formula that will save the planet! Allow your list to evolve throughout the day, and be prepared to let some things flow into the next day or week.

When you are really trying to get a lot done in a short amount of time, try to break down the list into blocks of time and/or geographic areas. For instance, go to three stores that are in the same vicinity on one trip. In these fuel-conscious times you will also save gas!

Judie has a unique To Do list technique. She doesn't care how many lists she starts…she just has them floating around. Sometimes she actually finds them and uses them. Her favorite thing is to find several, compare them, and cross off all the completed tasks. What could be more satisfying than to see everything you've accomplished in print?

You can also have To Do lists for long-term goals, such as painting the garage, cleaning out your storage bin, re-upholstering the couch. The act of making the list is often in itself a valuable tool. You don't need to be tied to it, because mentally you've focused on what you need to do. A lazy approach is to use it for organization, but not let your life be ruled by your To Do list.

SHOPPING

"Shopping is a woman thing. It's a contact sport like football. Women enjoy the scrimmage, the noisy crowds, the danger of being trampled to death, and the ecstasy of the purchase."

– Erma Bombeck

Do you love shopping a little too much? Are you addicted to online shopping, or the Home Shopping Network? Do you get so many catalogues that your mail carrier can't fit them in your box? Everytime you enter a store do you have to purchase something? Judie's daughter, Lisa, made this revealing statement about discount/warehouse shopping: "I'm good at the purchasing, but I'm bad at everything that comes after. I'm not even good at getting it out of my car and into my house." Some people buy so much they don't even remember what they've bought.

Or, do you hate shopping? Is your closet full of clothing that other people gave you? Is your underwear shot, but you can't bring yourself to go into a store to get new lingerie? It's hard for a lot of people to be balanced about spending money. Many overspend, as is evidenced by the enormous credit card bills our country is racking up. But others have a difficult time spending money on themselves or others. If you do, but under-spending isn't causing a problem in your life, then don't worry. Don't let the teasings of your relatives and friends get you down. Shopping is not a measure of your worth as a woman. But, if you feel unworthy of indulging yourself, try to treat yourself at least once in a while.

Overspending creates all sorts of problems. It isn't lazy to run up debt. It creates a financial burden, and becomes another source of stress. If you have "buttons" around shopping, pay attention to where you spend money or what causes you to buy impulsively. These are your danger zones.

We all have to take our own temperatures about the role shopping plays in our lives. Do you go out and buy something when you break up with a guy? When you are feeling overwhelmed or under-loved, do you overbuy? Whether it's jewelry, shoes or books that you buy with abandon, you need to take an honest look at your spending habits. If shopping is creating serious problems, financially or in your relationships, you may need to seek counsel, as these issues can have some significant underpinnings. Check out Debtors Anonymous (an offshoot of Alcoholics Anonymous). It's hard to avoid shopping entirely. We all have to shop – even if it's just for groceries. Beyond that, the level of time and effort it takes to shop can be significant.

Sometimes, even if you love to shop, it can become a burden just because it's never-ending. Note that the more particular you are about what you buy, the more effort it takes. (See the Lazy Woman's Practical Tip #1: "Use what you have.") You can even avoid a trip to the market, the hardware store or the dry cleaner just by getting creative about using what you have.

LAZYQUICK TIPS
How to be a Good Shopper

BULK

Bulk shopping saves time and money. Even if you are single, you can save on household items – and you can't beat it for a party. Watch out, though, for the "great deals" that cause you to spend more on impulse buys than you save on essentials.

ONLINE

We've personally never heard of an online purchase going awry, but you can check any online vendor at bizrate.com to see if they are viable. The best thing about online shopping is that you can do it in your pajamas at any hour of the day or night.

SALES

Use them but don't abuse them. These can be the Lazy Woman's helper or demise. Beware of those items which are almost perfect (i.e. need altering, a little reupholstering, etc.), but end up never making it out of the garage or closet. For clothing, if you check out the sale racks when you aren't under a lot of pressure (ie., without time or money constraints), you will make better choices. Ask yourself: Does it fit perfectly? Will

continued...

I have to buy a bunch of stuff to make it wearable? Even if it's a great buy, if it's never used, you will still have to pay for it, store it, and eventually get rid of it.

Discount/Remainder Stores/Thrift Shops

Many wonderful gems can be unearthed at the tackiest of stores. But you have to enjoy the process to make it worth time there. It's almost like a hobby or an indulgence that you fit in when you can: searching for the pearl amidst the oysters. It's not a good place when you need something specific in a hurry, because you never know what you are going to find.

Gifts

Gift giving should not be a burden. One of the ways to take some of the pressure off is to buy ahead. When you see something you know your sister, mother, husband, or best friend would love, buy it ahead. Have *one* place in your cupboard, garage, or attic where you keep these presents stashed.

You can also keep more generic gifts on hand for last-minute events or parties. Sometimes, they can end up as a special touch in a gift basket. For example, keep on hand scented soaps, mini-books, stationary, bubble bath or any of your favorite items. A small gift, a cake or plant can create a nice "cheer up," "happy birthday", or "I love you" gift.

LAZYQUICK TIPS
Quick & Easy Gifts

GIFT KIT

Gather blank cards & tags, a hole punch, different kinds of ribbon, paper, and fabric. With just these few "ingredients," you can create a gift for anyone!

FLOWERS

Grab flowers out of your garden or personalize store-bought (cut or potted) flowers. Take a scrap of fabric, wrap it around the stems (or pot), take a piece of ribbon and wind it around the fabric. Tie a bow and you have a beautiful gift, which is more personal and unique than a florist's.

GIFT ON ORDER

If you tried to buy a certain item, but it was out of stock or unavailable or just too darned far away to get to, cut out a picture of the gift (catalogue or magazine) that you will give the person, put it in a box and wrap it up as a "gift on the way."

GIFT CERTIFICATES

Make a "gift certificate" for dinner and a movie, a massage, a picnic in the park, day at the beach, car detailing, concert ... anything that you know the person would truly love and that you can easily make happen.

You can present it simply on a plain piece of paper in an envelope (or wrap it up in a box) or if you have a few extra minutes, you can get a little more creative with your presentation. For instance:

PICNIC: Wrap certificate in a napkin and tie it up like a mini-knapsack.

DAY AT THE BEACH: Take a beach towel or bottle of sunscreen and tie with a ribbon. Attach a tag that says "Redeemable for a Day at the Beach."

DINNER AND THE MOVIES (OR A PLAY): Make a gift certificate, for a particular restaurant, play or movie, by cutting out a review or advertisement. Put it in a card with a note. Or you can get fancy and attach it to a bouquet of flowers or a single rose.

The certificates can be as descriptive or as simple as you wish. It's the personal touch that counts.

HOLIDAYS

If hearing the word "Holidays" makes you break out in a sweat or gives you a knot in your stomach, you are not alone. Many people see holidays as fraught with family tensions and overwhelming demands, or as an unattainable image of perfection reinforced by media pictures. Even if you eagerly await that jam-packed end of the year holiday season, the intensity of the events and preparations can wipe you out. Either way, Lazy Women don't want tension and fatigue to steal their chance of experiencing some truly beautiful moments.

You may dread the guilt or feel you'll get too much flak if you don't join the family celebration, but the bottom line is you have a choice. (See Choices in Chapter 7.) Once you've made the choice, don't let your mind chatter spoil the holiday. You may have to let go again and again, but be wherever you are, free of guilt or resentment. This will allow the holiday spirit in.

"No self-respecting mother would run out of intimidations on the eve of a major holiday."

– Erma Bombeck

What if you could wave a magic wand that would create your idea of a perfect holiday celebration? Who would you spend the most time with, or the least? When you are visualizing this, try to be specific about where you would be, what it would look like, how long you would be there, where you might go afterwards.

With this picture as a starting place, create a holiday plan. You may not be able to have it all, but having an awareness of what you would truly like is the place to start. Sometimes we are so programmed to follow family and societal traditions, we aren't even aware of what might be most satisfying to us. Try to be open to new holiday experiences. See what you are drawn to after you wave that magic wand. You may be surprised that you can take care of yourself *and* meet your family obligations!

Judie: *For years after my father died, Thanksgiving was a mixed bag. My mother had several boyfriends through the years and Thanksgiving always included "the guy" and sometimes his family. I had three pre-teen daughters who didn't find this particularly attractive. Nor did my husband and I find it a particularly easy time. In order to make this more palatable for ourselves, our family of movie lovers carefully picked out a special movie. That way, we could be more cordial to the assembled bodies at Thanksgiving dinner because we had something fun to look forward to. Going to a movie on Thanksgiving evening has remained (even though my mother is now happily married) a special holiday tradition.*

When all else fails, remember Lazy Woman's Commandment #1 "This Too Shall Pass." The goal, though, is not to just survive the holidays, but to actually enjoy them.

Even when you *are* in the spirit, using shortcuts to make holiday preparations simpler leaves you with more energy to actually celebrate.

LAZYQUICK TIPS
Holiday Smorgasbord

FAMILY: Spend the day totally with your family, partially, or if they're terminally toxic, not at all. *You* decide based on your family history, your tolerance at the time, and what you can negotiate.

NEW TRADITIONS: Have your holidays become a burden? Be open to change. For instance, Judie, her family, and Bridget took off on the spur of the moment on Christmas night one year to drive up the coast to a peaceful ocean-side retreat. It was thrilling to be on the road when no one else was, and meet other people at the lodge, hearing about how they too came to be there on Christmas night.

ESSENTIAL INGREDIENTS: When some of the things you picture as vital to your holiday, like elaborate decorations or home-baked cookies, become such a chore that you can't wait until the holiday is over, it's time to edit the list of what's "essential". Make sure that the things you keep are the things that feed your soul and the spirit of the holidays.

DECORATIONS: Give yourself permission to *not* display all your decorations every year. Whether you choose yourself, or include your family in making the choices, just remember it doesn't have to be *everything*. Small touches can have a big impact.

LAZYQUICK TIPS
Kindling the Winter Holiday Spirit

PUBLIC EVENTS

There are plenty of free concerts, holiday shows, tree or menorah lighting ceremonies in most cities. You can go and feel a lot of love when so many are gathered in celebration.

VOLUNTEER

Even if it's just for a half hour to read a holiday story to a group of kids or to help decorate the neighborhood rest homes, giving time to others who are in need has a way of kindling warm holiday feelings.

GIFTS FOR PEOPLE WHO WOULD NEVER EXPECT A GIFT FROM YOU

Take a box of doughnuts to the local firehouse, leave candy or cookies and a holiday card for your letter carrier or your elderly neighbor. Giving unexpected gifts has a way of making *you* feel like you got a wonderful gift…and you did!

LAZYQUICK TIPS
Holiday Decorations

KEEP IT TOGETHER! Keeping all your holiday decorations together will save you a lot of time and energy. Put small decorations or knick-knacks in boxes clearly labeled "Hanukkah," "Valentine's Day," "St. Patrick's Day," "4th of July," etc. so that you don't have to buy new stuff every year or spend time finding things.

IT'S THE LITTLE THINGS. You can create a big holiday splash by clustering pine cones, candles, figures, lights, etc. in one area. You don't need to decorate the entire house. Put out a few things to add some festive cheer. Whether it's a few carved eggs, wooden bunnies, glass hearts or little Halloween figures on a mantel, windowsill or set around a centerpiece. Put out a couple bowls of beautiful fruit or favorite holiday candies. Accents don't have to be elaborate, handmade, or labor-intensive.

USE WHAT YOU HAVE. Incorporate your decorations with what is already in your home. Make it seem a part of the room decor. Nestle some Santas and snowmen in among the framed photos and collectibles on your shelf. Put holiday colored candles in the candelabras and candleholders that are already there. In other words, you don't have to clear away any part of your decor to accommodate the holidays. Let the holidays accent your decor and save time.

Make Me Up and Spit Me Out

A LAZY LOOK AT HEALTH AND BEAUTY

Beauty

Clothes

Diet

Exercise

Health

Aging

Menopause

PMS

Insomnia

INTRODUCTION

It all starts with "dress up." Clomping around in mommy's delicate sling-backs, tripping on pearls that touch our knees, rubbing lipstick far beyond the reaches of our tiny lips, we look in the mirror and see the most beautiful "woman" on the planet. Soon we are old enough to look at pictures in magazines and, later, to read the articles. Mommy isn't the only model for us now.

We receive messages from the media telling us the "shoulds" about our bodies -- how we should look, smell, feel, age, exercise, build muscles, eat, take care of ourselves, improve ourselves, love or not love ourselves -- all in the quest to be attractive to others. In the end we don't even know if these images reflect our individual needs, wishes, or tastes. We blindly accept them, as if the images will make us desirable.

As adults, some of us continue to feel like we are "dressing up." The pearls still seem to be dangling below our knees, but now, instead of feeling like our clothes are too big, we feel they are too small. The fantasy time awakened by playing dress-up has transformed into an internal image-monitor that haunts us.

How do we recapture that innocent and lazy way of loving our bodies and the thing we call beauty? We need to honor ourselves exactly as we are right now, to see ourselves as perfect. Anything less than that catapults us into the past, or drags us into the future. A Lazy Woman takes care of herself in this moment, instead of berating the past, or obsessing about an image she is striving blindly to achieve.

This doesn't mean that there isn't room to improve or challenge ourselves. When we forgive our bodies their flaws (real or imagined), we have energy and enthusiasm to approach genuine health and well being. Give yourself a gift: appreciate yourself now like you did when you looked in the mirror and thought you were the most stunning creature on the planet. You are. You are perfectly and wonderfully you.

BEAUTY

This was a hard section of the book for us to tackle. We both know the discomfort that comes with assessing our attractiveness, having our beauty fade, and trying to live up to societal standards. We have mental pictures of what we should look like, which vary through the years. The pictures are always hard to match.

Bridget and Judie believe in "Moments of Beauty" – the times in life when the flaws magically fall away and all is right from the earrings to the toes and we feel "hot!" Sometimes these moments continue for a long period of time. Other times, they are snapshots – maybe just moments – when you catch your reflection in a mirror and think, "I look great!"

This feeling of being beautiful (or not!) is exactly that – a feeling, sometimes based on reality, but most often not. As astounding as it may seem to most of us, even supermodels say the same thing. *Feeling* beautiful is what we care about. It's not as if we need to win a beauty pageant. We just want to feel like we made the semi-finals.

Bridget: *I frequent a spa which is known for its healing sulfur spring. I've been many shapes and sizes over the years and have noticed the various body types of others. When I first bare my naked body – yikes – I am self-conscious. But after a while, I start to see the beauty of each and every body. In fact, some of the most beautiful ones are even more round and Rubenesque than mine. I am not saying I don't cringe and wish I could hide when I see a model. But I definitely see the beauty of all feminine forms and end up appreciating my own more.*

*" Beauty...is something felt, a glow
or a communicated sense of fineness. What
ails us is that our sense of beauty is so
bruised and blunted, we miss all the best. "*

– D.H. Lawrence

The continued pursuit of trying to improve our looks, coming as close as we can to some imagined ideal, is futile at best, and always exhausting. If the pursuit of beauty doesn't bring you down, then you're well on your way to being a Lazy Woman. If, however, the beauty issue – whether it's your weight, skin, breast size, hair – still plagues you on a daily basis, you need to check out how much time and energy is going down the Beauty Drain.

If you spend 2 hours a day on beauty, that's over 700 hours a year...is it worth it? Keep it all in perspective and stay conscious of how much your beauty regime adds to or detracts from your well being.

LAZYQUICK TIPS

Mirror, Mirror on the Wall Who's The Laziest Beauty of All?

Little touches can make a big difference. Here are some low-maintenance ways to feel a little more beautiful.

LIPSTICK

It's amazing how the right lipstick can give a lift to your face. Some of the best instant enhancers are sheer natural colored lip covers. Remember, even the palest shimmer of lip gloss on the way out the door can make you look and feel better.

CONCEALER

A concealer that matches your skin tone blended around your eyes, and on any blemishes, evens out your skin and takes some time off your beauty clock — whether it's from lack of sleep or added years.

BLUSH

Give your face a light dusting of a natural color blush on the places the sun would kiss – cheeks, nose, chin and forehead. A little extra on the cheeks and you have a nice healthy glow.

So, what's the bottom line with beauty? There are three:

1. TAKE CARE OF YOURSELF: A healthy look is beautiful and sexy.

2. KEEP IT SIMPLE: Give yourself more Hammock Time. You can't apply make-up in the hammock, and you shouldn't want to!

3. HONOR YOUR OWN UNIQUE BEAUTY: We are so quick to acknowledge the beauty in our friends and family no matter what their physical idiosyncrasies. Include yourself: we are all beautiful creatures in our own right.

BEAUTY TIPS FROM THE ULTIMATE LAZY WOMAN: SLEEPING BEAUTY

Let's say that Sleeping Beauty drank a whole lot of **water** before she went to sleep (with the gift of not having to get up and pee in the middle of her sleep). Let's also say that little fairies gave her water throughout her beauty nap so that she was constantly being hydrated. Why? Because water and **sleep** are two beautifiers that you can never overdo. And, of course, Sleeping Beauty stayed out of the sun, because too much sun is a no-no – even for fairy tale characters! So the moral of our story: Sleeping Beauty gets plenty of rest, drinks a lot of water, and stays **out of the sun**

P.S. Note that Sleeping Beauty didn't need a lot of time or money to stay beautiful!

CLOTHES

Oy! What a mixed bag clothes are – pressure to look good, dress "appropriately," fit into things, buy the right things. We never have anything to wear, yet never have enough room in our closet for what we do have. There's a commercial with a woman coming home to her tiny apartment, squeezing through the tight spaces, and climbing over things to get to her closet which, it turns out, is an expansive, calm and gorgeous room – the haven of her home. She closes the door and sighs. She has arrived! Wouldn't we love to have a closet like that?

Most of us have to organize and edit, so that we have the space to move things around, see what we have, and quickly get to what we need. You've probably heard the rule of thumb that professional organizers give: If you haven't worn it in a year, throw it out. Well, it might be one year for you, or maybe two, but rarely any more. If it's a lovely fabric or a classic design, it may be worth hanging in the attic.

Judie's been around long enough to get a second life out of some of her great oldies, and her daughters are delighted with some of their mom's vintage goodies. Just make sure you have somewhere to stash these potential treasures, so they don't add to your clutter.

If your hang-up is how much you paid for something, it's easier to get rid of if you can give it to someone in need. Get out the phone book, and find a thrift shop that will pick up or go to www.dress-for-success.org, who provide for low income women trying to enter the job market. That way you not only clean out your closet and feel great but receive a charitable tax-deduction as well. Then, move the stuff that you don't use on a regular basis. Put it somewhere less convenient – an out-of-the-way closet or the garage. Put the things you use all the time in the most accessible spots, so you don't waste time looking.

LAZYQUICK TIPS
Clothes Horse
Win, Place or Show

COLOR YOUR WORLD SIMPLE

Choose a few basic colors that make you look and feel good. Interchangeable clothes make life easier. Use other colors as accents. Bridget wears a lot of black and white, but she buys funky colored shoes and scarves for accents.

EASY CARE

Avoid dry cleaning or ironing. Choose clothes that you just wash and hang up or throw in the dryer. You've got to truly love a piece of clothing to warrant a trip to the dry cleaner.

NOT TOO MANY FLOWERS, PLEASE

Save them for the tablecloths! Lots of patterned separates take time to match. For an easy classic look, solids are the way to go.

THE RIGHT TOUCH

Styles come and go each season, so don't be a slave to keeping up. Add accents to your basics to look hip. The right jewelry, scarf or "in style" shoe can make you feel oh-so-fashionable.

You want your clothes to enhance you *and* to be comfortable. Don't shove yourself into something that doesn't fit. It won't *feel* good, it won't *look* good, and you'll go through the day feeling like a sausage. It's not lazy to think about your clothes all the time – no matter how beautiful they are. Are gorgeous high heels worth it if you can't walk in them, or your back is going to be sore the next day? There are comfortable, well-designed alternatives out there. Why suffer?

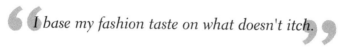 *I base my fashion taste on what doesn't itch.*

– Gilda Radner

Just like brushing your teeth, getting dressed is something you have to do every day. If you find that a "uniform" of sorts is what makes your life easier, then create some options for yourself. Create outfits that are nobrainers for you. Sometimes you don't want to even think about what to wear. Other times finding just the right thing is fun. The Lazy Woman is willing to shift gears in order to get out the door with a smile and a light heart.

Bridget has a friend who has no idea how to put an outfit together. She goes to stores and looks for the displays she likes that are completely done, with jewelry and all, and buys every piece. People always comment that she looks great, but she has nothing to do with the creation. It doesn't matter, though, because it makes her life easier, and she enjoys the compliments.

You control your wardrobe. Take charge and let *it* serve *you*!

DIET

Generally when we utter the word "diet," it's for one of two reasons: we want to feel better or look better. The old adage about feeling and looking good leading to doing well may have some merit. We all want to feel our best so that we can lead full lives.

Lazy Women want as much energy as they can get. The benefit of having more vitality is one heck of a reason to follow a good diet. Whether we are trying to lose weight or not, we can all choose to eat energy-enhancers (vegetables, fruits, whole grains) as opposed to energy-drainers (sugar, caffeine, starches).

If the thought of overhauling your eating habits is more than you can bear, just try sneaking in healthy alternatives. For instance, if you go for sugary snacks, *once in a while* try an apple or dried fruits; if you're hooked on chips, *once in a while*, grab a flavored rice cake and a slice of cheese instead. Slowly you can move toward a more healthy way of eating, without the burden or pressure of forbidding yourself favorite foods.

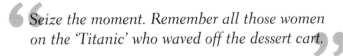

Seize the moment. Remember all those women on the 'Titanic' who waved off the dessert cart.

– Erma Bombeck

Don't make yourself crazy. Eating should be a pleasurable experience. If it makes you insane, it can't be good for you, no matter how nourishing the food might be. But this should not be confused with the ups and downs that can be associated with constantly changing your way of eating. In other words, if you are using food – particularly sugar and caffeine – like a drug, you may have some withdrawal symptoms if you cut back. These symptoms can be annoying and sometimes uncomfortable, but once they pass you will feel better.

So, what's a good diet? Every book has its own theory. You need to find a regime that works for the *long* haul – whether you are changing your diet to feel better or look better. Can you stay with it? If you develop an eating plan that is too extreme, you are bound to 1) fall off the diet and 2) go crazy with your eating when you do fall off.

Bridget has a friend who hates vegetables and fruits, so she can't follow most diets. She wants to lose weight, so it means she has to look a little harder to find an eating plan that suits her. She also needs to be sure to take vitamins to supplement her nutritional deficiencies. Tailor your eating plan to your tastes, issues, lifestyle, and emotional needs. What good does it do to choose a diet of brown rice and tofu if you know you'll never stick with it?

Besides *what* you're eating, look at *why* you are eating. Ask yourself: "Am I trying to push down a feeling with food?" Knowing and staying conscious of the emotions that cause you to overeat or eat unhealthy foods means that you can ask: "Is this going to make me feel good later?" and give yourself an honest answer.

At the same time that dieting and losing weight have become a national obsession, statistics are showing that Americans are becoming more and more overweight. Dieting is clearly having the reverse effect for at least some portion of the population. Each individual has to understand her own danger zones and the triggers to unhealthy eating. Once you know, you can start to live with awareness and develop strategies to move toward a more balanced relationship with food.

Whatever you have to do to help yourself stay on a healthier eating plan is worth it. Support groups like Overeaters Anonymous, and diet groups like Weight Watchers, have helped people realize that they aren't alone. Also, a plan that can slowly become an integral part of your life gives you a starting place. It may not sound lazy to keep a food journal, go to meetings, or measure your food, but if it's what you need to do to get the dieting load off of your shoulders, choose your weapon and do it!

LAZYQUICK TIPS
Know Your Food Traps

STEER CLEAR OF DANGER

You have to decide what "danger" is for you. Staying honest with yourself about the food issues you have, will help you avoid the aftermath.

SUGAR AND SNACKS IN THE HOUSE

Can you live with this stuff around or do you end up eating it? Bridget doesn't keep sugar in the house, because she'll eat it. She makes herself go out for it which makes her get conscious about what is behind the craving.

BUFFETS/SALAD BARS

Can you make healthy choices when faced with an enormous array of food? If weakened by vast food choices, give yourself some parameters – *before* you go.

PARTIES

Can you go somewhere where there is beautifully prepared and served food and not eat too much of the wrong stuff? Never go on an empty stomach.

DRINKING

Can you have alcohol and still have the fortitude to stay away from unhealthy foods? Sparkling water with

continued...

a festive twist makes you look like one of the grown-ups, but doesn't take the same toll on your body.

JUST DESSERTS

Some people do the bulk of their overeating at the worst possible time: after dinner. If you're truly hungry, or yearning for a sweet, choose a good snack. Popsicles or frozen fruit ices almost fulfill a mean ice-cream craving.

EXERCISE

You might think a Lazy Woman's book would suggest you avoid exercise. Not so! The lazy way to a long and healthy life includes at least moderate exercise. No one denies the benefits of exercise. It's all about making it a balanced part of your life.

If you hate exercise and can't stand the thought of fitting workouts into your weekly schedule, you need to figure out ways to sneak it into your life. A Lazy Woman starts by giving herself credit where credit is due. Do you clean your own house and/or garden? Do you walk your dog? Do you walk your child to school? Do you use stairs often during a normal day? Do you go dancing every week? In these cases, exercise is naturally built in to your lifestyle. Ideally, you want to exercise your heart a few times a week, do some strengthening exercises, and throw in a little yoga or stretching.

LAZYQUICK TIPS

Stealth Exercising:
Sneaking it into Your Day

WALKING: Look for ways to pick up extra mileage. Park further from your destination. Or, just open your door and walk. If you can't get up the motivation to walk alone, enlist a buddy or your mate. Meet between your houses and go on a walking adventure together! You can catch up on life while getting in a little workout.

STAIRS: Stairs are what 'Stairmasters' wanna be when they grow up. Avoid elevators when you can. Instead of complaining when you have to go back upstairs for things you forget, view it as time logged on your personal 'Stairmaster'.

GARDENING: This is a two-for-the-price-of-one endeavor. You eliminate weeds and get a workout too. Weeding, digging, raking, hoeing and dragging the hose around can elevate your heart rate if done with vigor, and will definitely strengthen your upper and lower body.

CLEANING: Vacuuming, sweeping, dusting and picking up all involve pushing, pulling, bending and squatting – the same things you do in an exercise class.

BABIES/KIDS/DOGS: Get out the strollers, leashes, and bicycles and hit the streets.

If you resist everyday activity, your lazy approach may be to join a gym or dance class, so that once you set a schedule or develop a routine, you don't have to think about it. Sometimes putting money into the equation can help motivate you too. Whatever program you begin, if you are uncertain about your health, be sure to talk to your doctor. There are so many exercise choices now. It's a matter of trying things until you happen upon a few that you can do with regularity. Fitness experts say that a varied program will keep your body balanced and your mind engaged.

We love a good yoga, muscle toning or Pilates class. These can cover all your exercise bases. You will get your heart rate up while strengthening and stretching muscles.

If you've never worked out before, it's not too late to start. Oprah did a show on women who were defying their age. One woman in her 80's was an award-winning weight lifter, who didn't start working out until she was in her 60's. Osteoporosis wouldn't even think of touching this woman. Her posture was impeccable, her strength amazing and her energy that of women half her age. Studies show that women who lift weights have better bone density.

If you can't or don't want to leave your house, but still want to feel like one of the workout crowd, get some videos, a yoga mat, hand weights, or a jump rope – whatever it takes to create your own living room gym. You can even buy a video online and never leave the house!

Make it happen. For every person there will be a different formula. The Lazy Woman finds a way to make exercise fit her world, but doesn't turn her world upside down to fit in exercise.

HEALTH

"I consider myself an expert on love, sex and health. Without health you can have very little of the other two."

– Barbara Cartland

Are you unconscious of the effects your daily choices have on your health? To some extent, most of us are or we would be hypochondriacs watching for every stomach pain, bump, or blister. Taking an honest inventory of your health, and the habits which affect it, is the lazy answer.

When so much information bombards you about the latest nutritional trends, toxic exposures, exercise crazes, wonder drugs and alternative treatments, it's hard to keep track of what's good and bad, much less incorporate it in your everyday life. There is no debating, however, the benefits of good health. Better health means more energy and who couldn't use more energy? Having healthy skin, hair, eyes, teeth, and muscles will take your appearance up a notch, too!

This is another one of those double benefits: you get to feel great now and your body will hold up better in the long run.

THE LAZY WOMAN'S HEALTH CHECKLIST

These are the basics. If you're not heeding them now, don't feel guilty. Just copy this checklist, tape it to your mirror and use it as your game plan for good health. Start today with at least one phone call to set up an appointment.

1. **Do you smoke?** Cut it out or at least cut back.

2. **Do you wear sunscreen?** It's an easy preventative. Fewer wrinkles or freckles and more cancer prevention.

3. **Do you keep track of the shape and color of any unusual spot or mole on your skin?** Get a chart from your dermatologist and use it to track any new spots or moles.

4. **Are you a couch potato?** Get up and move any way you can.

5. **Do you use drugs or alcohol?** Moderation.

6. **Do you have unsafe sex?** Not a good idea….ever!

7. **Do you give yourself a monthly breast exam?** Doesn't take a lot. Look in the mirror. Do they match? How do they feel? Anything new? Your doctor can give you a quick lesson on how to do a self-exam. Get to know your breasts and enlist your mate so that two of you are responsible for their future.

continued...

8. **Do you have a gynecological exam every year?** No excuses. Even if you're broke or uncomfortable, there are women's clinics that make it as easy as possible. Compared to the alternatives, this is a very lazy thing to do.

9. **Do you have a breast exam by a health professional at least once every three years (or annually if you are over 40)?**

10. **Do you have an annual mammogram?**

11. **Do you have a stool test for colorectal cancer if you are over 50 or if you have a family history of the disease?**

12. **Are you ignoring symptoms that could be warning signals?** Have you experienced sudden weight loss, blood in your urine or stool, abnormal spotting or cramping after intercourse or urination, black outs or chest pain?

13. **Do you have an annual dental exam and cleaning?** You can actually have major health problems caused by unhealthy teeth and gums.

14. **Do you take a good multiple vitamin?** No matter how well you eat, vitamins are insurance.

Check off items on this list as you make the small changes necessary to achieve better health. You can get a Pap smear, breast exam and colorectal cancer test in one doctor's visit. The same doctor can set up a mammogram and recommend a good multiple vitamin – **that's 5 for 1!**

LAZYQUICK TIPS
Happy Health

WATER: You can never drink too much water. Carry it with you; otherwise you end up passing several hours without it. When you do drink a lot – 3 liters a day – you have great skin, better elimination, and more energy.

LAUGHTER: Good for the face muscles. Even better for the spirit. Studies show that when you laugh you're improving your immune system.

EXERCISE: Do you need to be reminded? See Exercise

RELAXATION: Just sit down with a cup of tea and a book. In other words, give yourself a break. Find the nearest hammock.

PLAY: Whether it's with your pet, child, friend or on your own, engage with something or someone in a playful way.

MEDITATION: Sit down and pay attention to your breath – the sound of it, feeling your chest rise and fall. If you need something else to focus on, put on calming music or light a candle. Don't expect your thoughts to cease, but you may feel some relief. There is no "wrong" way to meditate, but, if you want some support, there are

continued...

many places to learn specific techniques. (See Lazy Woman Resources) Tapes can introduce you to a practice and give your mind something calming to focus on.

MASSAGE: Whenever you can, however you can... Massage is a renewing therapy to get you in touch with your body's own natural rhythm and energy.

SLEEP/NAPS: There is increasing evidence that beauty sleep and siestas contribute to overall health. What better reason do you have to get more sleep and take naps? What a luxurious, lazy way to improve your health.

X-RATED HEALTH

TYLENOL AND ALCOHOL: You'd never think this combination could be lethal, but a large dose can cause serious liver damage. The best policy is to avoid Tylenol when drinking.

MOST DRUGS AND ALCOHOL: Seriously, combining alcohol with just about any prescription or non-prescription drug is a no-no.

BUTTER AND BURNS: Butter or grease of any kind actually raise the temperature of your skin. You need to cool a burn. Cold water is ideal.

AGING

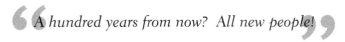

A hundred years from now? All new people!

– Anne Lamott

Aging is a fact. It's what you do with it that counts. Your attitude about it is everything.

We all know people who aren't aging easily or well, who are constantly whining about their age and fussing over it – no matter how old they are. They want to cover it up or do anything they can to stop it. Their life is a struggle to resist the inevitable.

Then there are those who just seem to move through the years, not denying their age, but not focusing on it either. They seem to have the attitude that aging is a natural progression, neither negative nor positive. The result is a person who is not only nicer to be around, but often seems younger than their years.

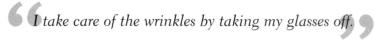

I take care of the wrinkles by taking my glasses off.

– Diane Sawyer

How you deal with aging is always a choice. (See Choices in Chapter 7.) You don't choose once and then you're done. Over and over, moment-by-moment, whenever your thoughts (or someone else's) trigger judgment about your age, you have a choice.

Judie: *When I was excitedly telling a friend that I was about to turn 50, she gasped and said, "Don't ever say*

your age, because then you will give it power!" I thought
about it for a minute, and then responded, "But I just
meant it as a number!"

And, I did. I marvel at the numbers. Sometimes I
say: "Can you believe I am this old? How amazing that I
got here. I feel like a kid!" Other times, like when I am
trying on clothes in a store, for instance, and I happen to
notice my wrinkling skin in the three-way mirror, I am
shocked. So, I make a choice: I take off my glasses so I
CAN'T see the flaws.

Whenever something triggers judgment about your
age, you can either get trapped in the endless inner
debate about aging, or you can choose for the moment
to put it aside. You don't have to decide to *never* be
depressed. We recommend procrastination (see
Procrastination in Chapter 7) when it comes to negative
thoughts about aging. Tell yourself you'll worry about it
later! Put it on your "To Do" list! (Apply this method to
anything upsetting or even slightly negative in your life.)

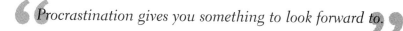

Procrastination gives you something to look forward to.

– Joan Konner

There's another reason why you can choose *not* to
fight aging. Aging can have unbelievable benefits. Most
people, if given a choice, would not go back to their
youth and give up the wisdom and insight they have
gained from their life experience.

Judie: *I would not trade places with Bridget, my own daughters, or any 25, 30, or 35 year old. Yes, I am coping with the wrinkles, menopause, sagging skin, weight fluctuations and creaky joints – the aesthetic and functional difficulties of aging. But I find I like my life better as I age. What used to bother me is no longer important. I look back on what used to stress me out and I have to smile. And, the more I have to look back on, the more I realize, "this too shall change."*

Yes, being closer to death is a piece of growing older. But being more focused on the good stuff that aging brings, instead of complaining about the wrinkles, is what creates a more contented life.

> *This is a youth-oriented society, and the joke is on them because youth is a disease from which we all recover.*

– Dorothy Fuldheim

How much time do you spend trying to "cover up" your age? There are a lot of things you can do with very little effort that will make you *look* younger. For instance, smoking, eating poorly, and spending a lot of time in the sun age us. So try to limit your exposure. Also, people who exercise regularly, drink a lot of water, do relaxation techniques (like yoga) tend to look younger, and they retain their energy and flexibility.

On the other hand, becoming *obsessed* with hanging on to your youth through extreme diet, compulsive exercise, or even plastic surgery, is *not* the Lazy Woman's Way. There are little things, though, that if done consistently, can reap lovely benefits.

LAZYQUICK TIPS
Dealing with Physical Aging

TAKE OFF YOUR GLASSES

Literally and figuratively. Don't look at all the signs of aging under a magnifying glass.

APPLES AND ORANGES

There's no way to feel good about yourself when you are comparing your image to that of younger women.

STAYING ACTIVE KEEPS YOU YOUNG

There are little lazy choices that can help you pick up exercise during your week – See "Stealth Exercising" in Exercise

AVOID EXTREMES

"Too big, too bright, too baggy, too tight" – the basic "If Dr. Seuss Were a Lazy Woman Fashion Formula" applies! Don't overdo it with hair, make-up, or clothing! The simpler the better.

CLOTHING

Pick a few favorite colors that make you feel and look good and stick with them. Choose cotton over polyester. You don't need to dress "old." You can adapt current trends to be appropriate and attractive. But, again, simpler is always better.

continued...

HAIR

Don't get stuck with a new version of your 80's hair style. Consult a stylist for the simplest, least labor-intensive style.

MAKE-UP

Stick with what nature gave you: choose sheer make-up, as opposed to heavy layering. Judie mixes foundation with some sunscreen moisturizer in the palm of her hand when she wants to create a healthy glow. A general rule of thumb is to use more subtle make-up with lighter clothing and a little more intense make-up with deep and dark colors. Avoid sparkling or iridescent colors (unless it's New Year's Eve!).

MENOPAUSE

Menopause is no longer something that happens toward the end of a woman's life cycle. The average life expectancy for a woman is 78, the average age that she enters menopause is 52. That means *one third* of a woman's life will be post-menopausal! The old stereotypes of menopause representing the end of the active, vital, sexual time of a woman's life have been replaced. With attention to diet and exercise, this phase gives women a whole new lease on life. No more unintended pregnancies, menstruation, or any of those monthly issues! Also, it turns out, post-menopausal women are the least likely to be depressed.

> " *Going to Hollywood to talk about menopause was a little bit like going to Las Vegas to sell savings accounts.* "
>
> – Gail Sheehy

As with other life transitions, the easiest way to navigate through it is to embrace it. There are ways to prepare for menopause, and ways to ease the symptoms as they occur. Probably the most debated treatment is hormone replacement therapy (HRT). Most American doctors recommend it to their patients, even when they are not experiencing symptoms. They advise that HRT will ease symptoms, help prevent osteoporosis and lessen the risk of heart disease. Doctors from other countries are more cautious, warning of potential side effects from

HRT: bloating, irritability, breast tenderness, headaches, and increased risks of breast cancer, blood clots, gall bladder, and liver disease. Even recent U.S. studies show mixed results for helping prevent coronary disease. Don't let your doctor's "just-do-it attitude" rush you into HRT. There are natural means to help you manage menopause.

Judie, with a father who died of heart disease and a mother who had breast cancer, chose not to use HRT. She pays extra attention to what she eats, uses dietary supplements, herbs, and takes her vitamins faithfully. She includes yoga, vigorous gardening, and running the stairs in her house as the basis of her exercise program.

If you've tried natural remedies without success and you're still bearing the burden of headaches, hot flashes, and/or other irritating symptoms, check out all your options and then do what works best for you. There are different types of HRT regimes and some specific hormone creams for vaginal dryness. Don't feel like a failure if you have to take hormones. Do what it takes to feel good.

A friend of Bridget's was unusually depressed soon after beginning menopause. She had recently lost a dear friend and thought she simply hadn't bounced back from the loss. Soon, though, the depression became worse and she went to a doctor who found her estrogen levels were extremely low. She now sings the praises of the estrogen "patch" her doctor gave her. When dealing with menopausal symptoms, remember Lazy Woman Commandment #1, "This too shall pass."

LAZYQUICK TIPS
Meandering through Menopause

DIET

Try to stick with a low-fat, high-calcium diet. There are a growing number of cookbooks with recipes for a menopause/post-menopause diet. The key additions are soy and other phytoestrogens (which means "estrogen from plants"). These isoflavones not only ease hot flashes, night sweats, and weight gain, they also may help prevent heart disease and osteoporosis.

DIETARY SUPPLEMENTS

- You can find the major isoflavones of soy (genistein and daidzein) in capsule form.
- Black Cohosh can help with hot flashes and vaginal dryness.
- Dong Quai is an herb that seems to help balance the female hormonal system and reduce stress.
- Chasteberry is often recommended by European doctors to help with symptoms of PMS and menopause.
- Red Clover has four important dietary isoflavones.
- Vitamin E, Calcium, Magnesium, and Vitamin D are important to have in your vitamin supplements.

LAZYQUICK TIPS

Menopause Helper – Make Soy Your Friend

Soy is recommended as a wonderfully natural way to put estrogen back in your system.

SOY-A-CUE: Sauté some onions in olive oil. Add tofu chopped into one-inch chunks. Throw in some of your favorite barbecue sauce and voilà: yummy tofu. Serve over mashed potatoes, baked potato, or rice.

SOYBEANS: Most frozen food sections have frozen soybeans (or "edamame"). Some fresh vegetable sections do too. Stick them in the microwave for a few seconds and enjoy!

TOFU "EGGLESS" SALAD/TOFU BURGERS/TOFU DINNERS: Check out your local health food stores and try some tofu goodies.

ROASTED SOY NUTS: They are a great snack. Toss them on salads, baked potatoes, or steamed vegetables.

SOY POWDER: Get soy protein powder and "sneak" it into your diet – a little bit in sauces or casseroles, and a hefty scoop in fruit smoothies and juices.

There are some wonderful books on the market about enhancing life *"pre* and *post"* menopause. There's no need to hurry. This is the rest of your life. Stop and smell the roses. Explore new ways of eating, new hobbies, new sports, travel and clubs…or just get out into the garden. Try the things you've been putting off – later is NOW!

PMS

If you are chronically debilitated several days every month with PMS, seek medical advice. If your doctor dismisses your complaints, then find another doctor. It may take some looking, but actively seek advice and sources until you are satisfied. Don't rule out alternative medical approaches, like acupuncture and homeopathy. The Internet can also be a great tool: you can communicate with people who have similar problems, find out what they've done, and look up current medical research. It can give you relief just to know you are not alone.

LAZYQUICK TIPS
PMS Pacifiers

AVOID THESE FOODS

Why eat things that don't help? Sugar, caffeine and salt do not help PMS. Doctors also often recommend eliminating polyunsaturated fats.

EMBRACE THESE FOODS

Vitamin E and soy foods are pretty easy to add to your diet and they both have been linked to reducing menstrual problems. Try substituting soy for dairy whenever you can. The healthier you eat, the better you will feel, particularly around this time of month. Eat fruits, vegetables and grains.

EXERCISE

Sometimes you feel like the last thing you want to do is move, but often symptoms can be relieved by moving your body.

DRINK LOTS OF WATER

Before, during and after - it flushes your system.

VITAMIN B

It helps process estrogen, increases progesterone levels and enables the brain to make serotonin.

continued...

HOMEOPATHY/HERBS

Some helpful alternative remedies are: dong quai, chasteberry and Evening Primrose Oil. St. John's Wort can help with mood swings. Also look for the sublingual PMS remedies in the homeopathy section of your health food store.

HUMOR

Note the absurdity of the push-me/pull-you attitude which can come with PMS. We want to be hugged, yet we scream irrationally, and appear quite unhuggable! Try to step outside yourself and see how funny the insanity is! We're not saying drop it – we know you would if you could – just see the humor.

SEX/CUDDLING

Sex does two things: it relieves physical tension, and it gives you a little love, which we all need during PMS. Cuddling works too!

EXTRAS

Speaking of love, give yourself some "extras" during your PMS time: warm baths, massages, nice walks in the park, more R&R, etc.

GIVE YOURSELF A BREAK

Don't fight your PMS. Do all that you can to relieve your symptoms, but until they're gone, let it be OK that you feel different for a while. As with any issue, the more you fight it, the more miserable you will be...

INSOMNIA

*" I did not sleep. I never do when
I am over-happy, over-unhappy,
or in bed with a strange man. "*

– Edna O'Brien

The clock keeps ticking, your mind keeps racing. You are dead tired, yet you can't fall asleep. Sometimes you actually make it into dreamland when out of the blue the "sneaky sleep robber" wakes you up. Insomnia is one of the top ten reasons why people see doctors.

The "Catch 22" of insomnia is that it is often born of stress, yet it creates even more stress, thus beginning a never-ending struggle.

Judie: *I have been troubled by insomnia on and off for many years. The most reassuring thing for me when insomnia strikes is to grab onto the Lazy Woman's Commandment #1, "This Too Shall Pass." As with all stress and fear, if I look at the insomnia as a never-ending condition, it is overwhelming, and I feel paralyzed. The opening to a solution is in the knowledge that it truly will pass.*

LAZYQUICK TIPS
Escaping Insomnia

STRESS

Avoid dealing with anything stressful in the evening hours. Paying bills, dealing with difficult phone calls or situations, watching stressful television shows (i.e., the evening news) or movies can create an agitated state.

CLEAR YOUR MIND

For the thoughts that don't want to quit, keep a pad and pencil next to your bed and write down anything you're afraid of forgetting. If the thought comes back, remind yourself that you've written it down, and you'll deal with it when you wake up. Remember Scarlet O'Hara's wisdom: "I'll worry about that tomorrow".

FOOD AND DRINK

Avoid stimulants in the afternoon and evening (for some people all day): coffee, tea, chocolate, cola, nicotine, sugar, etc. will help keep you awake. Many people claim they aren't affected by stimulants like these, yet will confess they have a daily cup of caffeine in the early afternoon and can never get to sleep. You may have to write down your food and drink intake to get to the root of your problem. Also, we sometimes feel that alcohol relaxes us for bed, and while initially it might,

continued...

chemically it metabolizes into sugar after a couple of hours and can actually wake us up.

EXERCISE

Exercise in the evening can keep you awake, but exercise earlier in the day can actually help you sleep at night.

RELAXATION

Use relaxation helpers: hot baths before bed to relax your muscles, and relaxing music and meditation tapes, to calm the mind. Listening to a soothing voice speaking reassuring words can induce relaxation.

BODY TEMPERATURE

Studies show that your body temperature affects your sleep. That's why a warm bath to raise your body temperature before bed is a good idea. You can try wearing socks to bed too.

PERSONAL RHYTHMS

Some of us just aren't meant to sleep straight through every night or be in bed by 11 p.m. and up at 6 a.m. Your sleep pattern may even run in your family, so make peace with it, and develop strategies to manage it.

If you haven't been able to fall asleep or stay asleep throughout the night for over a month no matter what changes you've made in your lifestyle or diet, it may be time to consult a sleep disorder specialist or therapist.

Lazy Women don't have time to suffer sleeplessness. There are many creative new techniques to help people reset their body clock with light therapy, etc.

Judie's doctor discovered that the racing heartbeat that often kept her awake was caused by a mitral valve problem. Sometimes the only way for her to calm this condition is with medication. If a physical or emotional crisis is keeping you awake, do not rule out talking to your doctor about medication. Sleep is crucial to a lazy life.

Have faith: there is a solution. You may figure it out very quickly or you may need help, which could come in the form of a medical or holistic doctor, stress-reduction or meditation techniques, or a new eating or exercise plan. Know that there is help out there. Keep trying things. In the meantime, try to relax and catch naps when you can.

Please, God, Deal Me a New Hand

SIMPLY AND SANELY DEALING WITH LIFE

Moods & Emotions

Undo

Self-Esteem

Stress

Quickies

Procrastination

Perfectionism

Birthdays

Anger

Choices

Envy

If Only

INTRODUCTION

What to do, what to do? When you're having an awful, no-good moment, and feel like you need divine intervention, where do you start?

It can be an emotional pit with your mind frantically searching for a way out. Sometimes, it's the daily logistics of how to get it all done, or the struggle to consider every aspect of a decision. You may go for years with the same unmade decisions weighing you down, waiting to find the last piece of the puzzle before you act.

Life is like a jigsaw puzzle. The pile of pieces don't make much sense, and you wonder where to begin. It only makes sense when you complete the puzzle: "Oh, I see, that piece was part of the tree," or "That looked like an edge piece but wasn't." Usually, you don't remember the frustration of when you were stuck and only see how logically the pieces now fit together. Often, we have the same experience when we look back at a resolved issue or period of time in our lives. Sometimes, we even realize that an event we thought was too painful to survive has actually enriched us.

If we can keep reminding ourselves that it will fit together in the end, then we can accept that part of the process is *not* knowing. Letting go of the need to know, the pieces fall into place as you move through life. You don't need to force them, because sometimes it's not an edge piece, it's part of the sky.

CHAPTER SEVEN

MOODS & EMOTIONS

Bridget: Judie suggested I take a stab at writing this section. I didn't take offense, though, because she was right to let me take the first look at it. I am probably the moodiest person I know. I am definitely the easiest to be brought to tears, wearing my emotions on my sleeve. I have an annoying obsession with honesty as well, so being honest about how I "feel" is one of my most urgent priorities. It has gotten me into trouble many times. I am therefore awed by Judie who is not dragged around by her emotions. I keep hoping "growing up" will get me to where she is, but I'm afraid that no matter how hard I work on myself, I will always lead with my heart, never my head.

Emotions are part of being human. For some people, the impact of feelings on daily life is minimal, for others, it is the dominant thread. Some experience erratic moods during certain periods, like after a trauma, break-up or death. Even happy changes like marriage or the birth of a child can trigger an emotional roller coaster. Being a slave to emotions, or a victim of self-inflicted emotional battery, is a full-time job. There's no energy left for anything else.

The goal is to experience your emotions, but not be ruled by them. Become aware of the role emotions play in your life and in the choices you make that impact your well-being. It could be as simple as not getting enough sleep, smoking and drinking too much, or not eating well. Are you setting yourself up for a fall? It's important to take responsibility for how certain actions affect your overall welfare.

If you are debilitated by emotions most of the time, you need to seek help. There are great self-help programs (e.g., Twelve-Step Programs, support groups), therapies, and pharmaceuticals. Some people need chemical balancing just as a diabetic needs insulin. If you are one of these people, you have to tend to this. Ask for support if you can't seek the help alone.

Sometimes it's impossible to separate your sense of self from your emotional state. But knowing that you aren't your emotions, that you are separate, gives you the ability to watch them from afar and even enjoy them. When your emotions are as at home within you as your blood and breath, you are truly in the flow of your life, which is the Lazy Woman's Way

> *Emotion doesn't travel in a straight line. Like water, our feelings trickle down through cracks and crevices...*
>
> – Sue Grafton, *I is for Innocence*

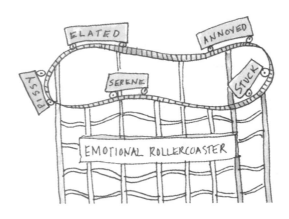

LAZY MOOD MODERATORS

DON'T BE A SLAVE! Do you spend time directing your life to either avoid a certain emotion or cater to it? Either way, you are enslaved.

BE HONEST. Are you addicted to your emotions? Are you a **drama queen**? Do you get sympathy for being depressed, angry, or sad? Does your anger give you energy? Do you get a little high from the attention you get from others? Being rigorously honest with yourself is the only way to get any relief or to affect change.

DON'T FIGHT THE MOOD. Take the third party approach to your emotions. **Stand back** and watch as much as possible. Sometimes a mood will lift sooner if you don't try to push it away. When you judge yourself, then you end up having yet another layer of guilt or anger on top of the original feelings. Fighting emotions, like fighting tears or hiccups, is a losing battle that only ends up giving you heartburn!

SEEK OUT PEOPLE WHO ARE NOT EMOTIONALLY CHARGED. If you are in an emotional state, surround yourself with people who are more **balanced**. It will make your life easier, because you won't be more agitated by their emotions!

DISTANCE. If there are important people in your life that add fuel to your emotional fire, try to get some distance from them when you're in an emotionally sensitive state. Just **leaving the room** for a few minutes can make the difference in heading off a clash or a meltdown.

Undo

If you use a computer a lot, you probably know about the "Undo" command. Computers allow you to undo, undo and undo – all the way back to where you started. In Microsoft Word, there is even a shortcut for it (one of Bridget's favorites), which is CTRL + Z!

The Undo command is a good metaphor for a Lazy Woman's life. On a daily basis, the best way to keep things in perspective is to realize that most things can be undone. Daily decisions that feel like they are the "be-all-end-all" generally are not.

There are very few things that can't be undone, even though you may have to pay a price in effort, dollars, or dignity to do so. When you embrace the Undo attitude, you will gain a great sense of freedom.

Self-Esteem

Self-esteem is only an issue when it is shaky. Specific actions can help reclaim or restore damaged self-esteem.

The media assaults our self-esteem on a daily basis. We are continually exposed to celebrity-saturated images of the ideal, healthy, beautiful, happy person. When we compare ourselves to this Celebrity Stew, we often come up short.

We all have Celebrity Stews, made up of media ingredients – pictures in magazines, sound bytes on TV, quotes in print – simmering in our mind's eye. Though these images seem very real, they give us false expectations of others and ourselves. "Why doesn't my husband look like

Brad Pitt?" or "I want Cameron Diaz's thighs." Therein lies the trap.

The trick is to realize that it is just a "stew" of random ingredients that you have allowed into the pot. Do a reality check. No one else's life is as perfect or pretty as the public advertisement. It's fine to admire or emulate someone's character or achievements, but use it as inspiration. Don't tie your self-esteem to it. Don't let the idealized version of someone else's life foster envy, depression, or ingratitude.

There are subtle self-esteem ripples and then there are peaks and valleys. If your self-esteem has been and continues to be at the bottom of your discontentment, then the lazy answer may be therapy. For the self-esteem fluctuations that are just part of the human condition, though, a little jumpstart every now and then can work wonders.

LAZYQUICK TIPS
Self-Esteem Builders

CUT YOURSELF SOME SLACK: Focus on the positive. Make a list of the things that you do love about your life or the way you look, like you love your toes, or the way your eyebrows arch, or the way you make an omelet.

TAKE AN HONEST LOOK: You know every one of your own fears and flaws. But, when you compare yourself with others, you only see the well-edited and groomed self that they present to the world.

DO SOMETHING FOR SOMEONE ELSE: Your self-esteem will be strengthened in proportion to what you give to others. It doesn't take much – a one-minute phone message left on someone's machine, or a smile and wave to a neighbor when you get the mail. Reach out to someone else: read your kid an extra bedtime story, surprise your husband with a cup of tea and his favorite brownie, call your mom just to say "goodnight," and let your dog sleep on the bed instead of the floor once in a while. It's hard to not feel better about yourself when you do something for someone else.

DO SOMETHING HEALTHY FOR YOURSELF: Even if it is just drinking a glass of water, or taking a short walk because you know it's good for you. It doesn't have to be big, but it's a gift for your body.

STRESS

We all have stress in our lives. Most of us would like to eliminate some of it. The first step is to identify the cause so you can clarify the things you can and cannot change. With the things you *can't* change, you can learn to manage their effect. With the things you *can* change, you need to decide what and how.

We work with some stresses better than others. For instance, mothers get used to crying children and waitresses adjust to the dinner rush. But some stresses are what we call INCOMING MISSILES. They catch you off guard and hit hard: out of the blue, your neighbor yells at you because your barking dog has been driving him crazy; you find out that the extended warranty on your car is worthless; or a relative calls begging you to bail out a troubled nephew you haven't seen in years. You can't anticipate an attack – and there may be several in one day – so, it's good to be prepared.

Whatever the cause of the stress, we need to be aware of when it moves into the "I-Can't-Take-This-Anymore" category. Sometimes the symptoms are physiological: rapid heart rate, shortness of breath, dry mouth, a desire to cry, queasy stomach, or listlessness.

Whatever triggers these symptoms, relief is necessary.

LAZYQUICK TIPS
Anti-Stress Arsenal

You need an arsenal of approaches to: 1) STOP the stressful thoughts, 2) CALM yourself and 3) REFOCUS your attention. In the case of a multi-missile strike, you may have to employ several counter-measures.

Alone time

Find a quiet place and let everyone know you need some time alone. If you are at work, you can always use a bathroom stall. Having this quiet time, away from stimulation, can sometimes allow you to more readily refocus your thoughts.

Get up and get out!

Change your environment and move your body: walk the dog, take a run, or take the kids to the park. Make yourself focus on the flowers, trees, and clouds. It's hard to stay in a contracted state when you are appreciating nature.

Have a cup of tea – or whatever calms you

The ritual of making tea and sipping it slowly tends to help slow our thoughts down. Some of our favorite calming herbal teas are Kava, peppermint, and chamomile.

continued...

Music

Put on your favorite relaxing music. Try to actually listen to it, letting it carry you away.

Take a bath or shower... and linger!

Feel water washing away every ounce of tension in your body. If you want to, proclaim out loud: "My stress is washing away..."

Homeopathics

There are wonderful natural products on the market that induce relaxation. Some of our favorites are Rescue Remedy, Flora-Calm, and Avena Sativa.

Meditative and Inspirational Tapes

There are many great tapes available. You don't have to DO anything, just listen. Some of our favorites are listed in the Lazy Woman Resources. Find one or two that you can always have at home, work, or in the car.

Hammock Time

Let the Hammock support *you*. Let yourself relax into it and look up at the trees.

Anything but YOU

Particularly if you can't get away and be alone, focus on anything but yourself: call a friend who would love to hear from you. Focus on the Lazy Woman Commandment #6, "Put your attention outside yourself."

Have your own effective stress-escapes ready in case you are caught off guard. If you cannot turn off stressful thoughts, seek help from another person. Call someone in your circle of friends, or a professional (a therapist, yoga teacher, or healer) – anyone that will help open the door to a calmer state. It's the Lazy Woman's Way to ask for help.

Give yourself time to recover and renew because after the source of the stress is gone, or minimized, you could still experience what we call a "Stress Hangover." So, continue using the "Anti-Stress Arsenal," and remember, "This too shall pass."

QUICKIES

Celebrate the quickie – whether it's a quickie wash in the laundry room or an intimate moment in the bedroom. Try not to judge that it isn't the full wash and dry cycle or a long, languid session of lovemaking. Love it for what it is – a shortcut to satisfaction!

PROCRASTINATION

Procrastination is usually perceived as a negative. In fact, it can be an art form or an albatross. The question is whether you'll pay a price for procrastinating and how *big* a price.

Some things have to be done, like medical/dental exams, taxes, bill paying, and feeding your family. Other things - like cleaning your closet, fertilizing the garden, or sending a thank you note - are not as pressing. Unless, of course, they are constantly on your mind, nagging at you. Then, the penalty is peace of mind.

> ❝ *But Jesus, you can't start worrying about what's going to happen. You get spastic enough worrying about what's happening now.*❞

— Lauren Bacall

PROCRASTINATING: THE ALBATROSS

Procrastinating becomes an albatross when the things you are postponing won't go away until you do them. Are you avoiding a breast exam or Pap smear? These are among the things that are *not* an option. You either do them or they will continue to nag you until you get them done. In this case, you need to *stop* putting it off and take action. Enlist help from a friend if necessary. Make one phone call. Take any single step to end the cycle of procrastination.

If it's something that can't be avoided, it's best to do the task when you think of it. The Lazy Woman's Way is to get rid of stress, not create it! Even if it's been on your "To Do List" for months, you can find relief by dealing with it.

Other commitments, choices, and promises become self-imposed problems. You tell your mother you are going to call her at a certain time. You don't call as promised and end up feeling irritated and guilty. You run the risk of finally making the call filled with resentment. Either let it go or force yourself to make the call. Make the choice and move on. It's the worry that creates the albatross.

PROCRASTINATING: THE ART FORM

Deliberate procrastination can be a useful tool. Look at the things that are weighing you down–like worry or self-imposed chores, and put them on your "To Do List." Promise yourself you will deal with them later.

Tell yourself "I *won't forget* this, I'm just not going to do it *right now*." Procrastination may be an indicator of good intuition. If you find yourself procrastinating and you don't know why, it might just be your intuition speaking. If there are no negative repercussions to putting something off, then just go with it. Often it ends up that a delay has saved you wasted energy, time, or money. Sometimes, it turns out that it was something you did not need to do or that it wasn't in your best interest.

> *Never put off until tomorrow what you can do the day after tomorrow...*
>
> – Mark Twain

LAZY QUICKTIPS
The Art of
Procrastination

MAKE PROCRASTINATION WORK FOR YOU

1. IDENTIFY WHAT YOU ARE PUTTING OFF.

2. WHY ARE YOU PROCRASTINATING? Fear? Anger? Resentment? The first step is to become aware of what stops you.

3. ASK YOURSELF WHAT PRICE YOU ARE PAYING FOR NOT DOING IT. If there is no penalty, let it slide, and see where it goes. It could just be good intuition guiding you.

4. IF YOU WILL PAY A PRICE, YOU JUST NEED TO TAKE ONE STEP. You may need to ask a friend to help you. Give yourself a pat on the back every time you take some action to end the procrastination!

5. YOU CAN PUT LOTS OF THINGS ON A MENTAL (OR REAL) "TO DO LIST," SUCH AS WORRY. If there is something you truly need to handle, it will still be there, with or without the worry. The worry doesn't bring any clarity or action, it just depletes energy. If you want to avoid eating certain foods, you can put them on your list to eat later. It is easier to accept "I will eat that candy later" than it is to struggle with "never."

PERFECTIONISM

Perfect marriage, perfect garden, perfect party … somehow we have all created our own ideal images. We go through life trying to match reality to these pictures.

Many people are proud of being perfectionists, but perfectionism can be a cross to bear, a self-imposed prison. When you are driven to be the ideal wife, mother, worker, etc. you are probably damaging yourself and those around you. When you drive your children too hard, expecting perfectly clean rooms, perfect grades, perfect behavior, it can become a burden they carry the rest of their lives. Also, where there is perfectionism, there is seldom creativity, spontaneity, or joy. Let go of your idea of what "PERFECT" is and see what you can tolerate. The Lazy Woman has the ability to enjoy the process and the result – no matter how it turns out.

BIRTHDAYS

Are you stressed out about your birthday? Do you have rules about your birthday? Does everyone know them? Do they change from year to year? Is your birthday always a drag?

> *You probably don't even look any more than twenty four hours older than you did yesterday. It's only your personal piece of hard luck that you are what you are today, when, inside, you never felt cuter.*

– Dorothy Parker, *The Middle or Blue Period*

Most birthday disappointments come from either not knowing what we want or not asking for it when we do know. There are very few people who genuinely want their birthday to be ignored. For some people, the smallest gesture – a simple "Happy Birthday" can make a difference. For others, their ideas are much grander. Bridget loves birthdays and believes in the "Birthday Festival" (preferably one week long) in which she pretty much gets to do whatever her heart desires. It may sound selfish, but how many times during the year do we really allow ourselves, without judgment, to do what we want to do?

It's a good idea not to wait until the last minute to figure out birthday desires. There is less chance of disappointment if you know in advance what you want, so that you can make it happen.

Judie takes the truly lazy approach to her birthday and is more or less happy with however it goes. She tries to get a little mileage out of it, even if it's buying something special for herself without any guilt. Try to appreciate whatever it is that people do for you, even if it's not what you had in mind. This is one time to remind yourself that it's the thought that counts.

Remember this also when dealing with other people's birthdays. Don't feel pressured to make all their dreams come true. You don't have to find the perfect gift or gesture. Overlooking someone's birthday because you aren't prepared makes them feel bad, and you feel guilty. The Lazy Woman is even prepared for forgotten birthdays. (See Gifts in Chapter 5.)

The single biggest symbol of the birthday is the *cake*. Since this usually has to be ordered ahead, it can present a problem if you forget about it. Never fear, the party cake is here.

QUICKIE PERSONALIZED BIRTHDAY CAKE

WHAT YOU WILL NEED: Store bought cake, Ribbon, Paper & Pen (or crayons), Candles, Fresh flowers

Discount markets sell big sheet cakes (or half sheets) that look plain, but are quite delicious and can often pass for homemade. (Bridget knows, she has served many and has been asked, "How do you have the time?!").

Take a thick **ribbon** (as wide as the cake is high) and tie it around the cake, leaving plenty of length on both ends so that you can tie a big **bow** in the front. You can add other ribbons for a more festive look.

For a **cake topper**, decorate with fresh **flowers**, draw a "Happy Birthday" sign, or cut up an old birthday card and stand the message up anchored in the frosting. Pop in the candles, light them and **sing**!

ANGER

We all have to deal with anger – our own and others. It's how you let it affect you that makes the difference. It's not lazy to let anger dominate your life. Undetected anger is like radon in your house, a silent killer.

Develop your anger detection system. Sometimes you don't realize that you're acting out of anger, or that someone or something is irritating you until you snap. Some anger is carried from so far in the past and you've lived with it for so long, that you figure it's part of your personality. Other people's anger is pretty easy to recognize if they express it overtly. When it's passive aggressive, it can be trickier to detect. However it's packaged, you need to recognize it and handle it, without either repressing it or dumping it on others, so that it doesn't shape your life.

Judie and her husband deal with anger in opposite ways. Jay is a "venter," and she is a "repressor." Early in their marriage, he would bait her when he was looking for a little arguing action, to vent frustration or stress. She would take the bait and engage in her side of the argument. One day when they were hurriedly trying to leave their house to catch a plane, Jay was railing and ranting about their always being late. Judie tried to make suggestions and defend herself. She realized that it didn't make any difference what she said. She chose to stop trying to "fix" the problem, and quietly finished her packing, while he continued his tirade. As they left the house, Jay said "Don't you have anything to say?" and she responded, "You're right, we should probably get ready earlier." A few beats later, Jay turned and said, "Well, this is no fun." It shifted the dynamic of their relationship. Even though their styles of handling anger remain the same, there is now the understanding that she doesn't need to engage or try to fix his anger. Sometimes he still tries to bait, but she doesn't often bite.

LAZYQUICK TIPS
Anger Detection &
Defense System
(Theirs)

VENTING: Even when you know that someone's venting doesn't have anything to do with you, you can still get plugged in. If you can recognize that you are not responsible for their feelings, you've won half the battle. From this detached state, you might be able to help them gain some insight into their anger, or at least not get dragged into an argument.

CRITICISM AND BLAME: When criticized or blamed you get defensive, justify your actions, feel attacked, sorry for yourself, or inadequate ("I never do anything right"), or maybe you simply shut down. Step back, unhook, take a look, and try to honestly listen to what they are saying. Often, just letting them know that you hear them diffuses their anger. This doesn't mean that you have to accept blame. But if there is something you see that you can do differently next time, it will be from this neutral perspective.

COVERT/REPRESSED/CONTROLLED ANGER: Don't expect them to admit it. It's a waste of time to try to get someone who is in denial about their feelings to admit that they are angry. Distance yourself emotionally and/or physically, if necessary. Save any meaningful discussions for a later time, when they might be more open.

LAZYQUICK TIPS

Anger Detection & Defense System

(Yours)

FEAR/JUDGMENT: Do whatever it takes to see that anger comes from fear and judgment. Some *thing* or *person* (even you) is not doing what you want them to do, or what you have "judged" that they should do. When you face the fact that you do not control things or people, you become afraid. Your mind then grabs onto the fear and churns out all sorts of judgments, e.g., "I can't stay married to someone who always..." or "I can't work with someone who..." This fear and judgment manifest themselves in anger, whose subtle disguises are frustration, irritability, and "snappishness."

"YES, I'M ANGRY:" Sometimes just admitting that you are angry can diffuse it, and then you can decide whether it is worth the energy it takes to stay angry. From this state, you can communicate with more ease and clarity.

IF COVERT/REPRESSED/CONTROLLED ANGER IS YOUR M.O.: Do you use anger to manipulate people? Early indicators are: talking through your teeth, clenched jaw, tight lips and clipped speech. When you are caught (kids are great at this!) or you catch yourself, do yourself a favor: don't get defensive, admit it, and try to lighten up.

LAZYQUICK TIPS
Anger Detection & Defense System
(Yours: When the Outside Agitators Get Inside)

These are things that can subtly wear you down, even when you're not aware of it. Traffic, incompetent salespeople, telemarketers, long lines in the market, computer glitches, etc. can get on your nerves. If you notice that things are getting to you, remember Lazy Commandment #1 "This too shall pass." Getting stuck in the mire of irritation is a waste of time. Let go and move on.

CHOICES

> "Each choice creates a future. It brings into being one of many possible futures. That is the future you will live in."

– Gary Zukav

The Lazy Woman realizes that how she chooses to spend her time, money, and emotional energy, affects the quality of her life. The outer choices range from what job to take, what man to marry, what house to buy, to what meal to cook, what errands to run, what dress to wear. Sometimes this means you choose once and it's over. Other times, it's an ongoing situation with a choice looming for a period of weeks or months. The latter is especially fertile ground for constant inner debate, asking the opinion of everyone around you, and otherwise driving yourself and others crazy looking for the right answer.

When you are weighed down by a particular decision, no matter how high the actual stakes, try to remember Lazy Woman Commandment #2, "Experience the moment you are living while you are living it." Instead of getting caught up thinking about how it's going to turn out in the end, make the most profound choice: do *not* *react* to what is happening around you – or inside your head!

You are actually creating your future opportunities by how you react to things now. When you make a choice, there are two things going on: *what is actually happening* and *your reaction*. But they aren't distinctly separate. Your reaction impacts what is happening, sometimes actually changing the outcome in a significant way. Beware: if you close a door out of anger or fear, you may be cutting off an opportunity that could change your life or, at the very least, impact the quality of your relationships and happiness.

You can learn to notice your emotional response to people and situations, and then you have a choice to *not* act out of those emotions. Life is much easier when you don't get sucked into someone else's emotional stuff – whether it's your toddler's tantrum, your boss' needling, or your friend's insensitivity.

When Judie's daughters were in their teens, and her oldest daughter was leaving for college, she had an experience of the power of letting go of her reaction.

Judie: *At the time I had been working with* The Course in Miracles *for several weeks. Always in search of the easiest way to do things, I had taken the advice given in the introduction about not trying to understand how the Course worked. My oldest daughter was moving out of the bedroom she had had to herself since she was 8. It seemed logical to let one of her sisters move into the coveted "private" bedroom, but this entailed moving the belongings of three teenagers. My mother was there to help. When tensions had reached a fever pitch, and nothing was being moved because of cries of, "I can't move my stuff until you get all that junk out of the closet!", Grandma sided with the girls and declared this an impossible task. I was getting sucked into their tense, "snappish" behavior, when I remembered to reach for my daily Miracle (being of hazy memory I carried it on an index card in my pocket.) I can remember the gist of it to this day: "My meaningless thoughts show me a meaningless world." I stopped what I was doing, read the card, pondered it for a moment, walked over to a pile of books, and moved them into the hall. With no attitude, attachment, or plan, I simply started moving things. Within minutes, everyone was working, and within an hour, much progress had been made and everyone was laughing. I realized then why it was called a* Course in Miracles.

Whether you use the *Course in Miracles* or not, if you can develop the ability to detach – even on the smallest level – it transforms your life. Doors open, avenues clear.

Being able to choose not to react out of judgement, anger, or irritation, allows you to be in the moment, and make the ultimate choice: happiness. As we say in Lazy Woman's Commandment #5, "You can either be right or be happy." It's your choice.

ENVY

Sometimes you can't believe it when you hear that someone is unhappy in a dream job, relationship, or house. Comparing yourself with others, though, is truly a waste of time. You never know how someone else's life really is. You just think you know. The relationship you envy, the lifestyle you covet, is created by assumptions you make about other people's lives, based on purely superficial observations. Think Charles and Di: for years everyone thought they had a storybook marriage.

Look underneath envy. Something else is always going on. Are you unhappy with your life, feeling that you are not getting what you need or deserve? All of us feel momentary envy, even if it's just the neighbor's new car. But when you get stuck fantasizing about having someone else's things or life, you've eliminated any possibility for enjoying what you do have. (See Gratitude in Chapter 8.)

The only smart thing to do with envy is to drop it when you notice it. Do whatever it takes to get a perspective on what it is you envy, and remember Lazy Woman's Commandment #3, "Take pleasure in what you have."

IF ONLY

We are haunted by thoughts of what we should have, should do, should be...the "Shouldsmare" – the Nightmare of Shoulds! "If only I had what I feel I should have..."

It takes a tremendous amount of emotional energy to live in a constant state of "If Only." Your thoughts have to be stuck in the past or projecting to the future, so there's no way to be in the present. You can only be truly happy and content experiencing the present moment, so "If Only" robs you of this potential.

"If Only" is one of the mind's favorite places to spend time; creating a world where *this* should have happened or figuring out how to make *that* happen. Sometimes, no matter how hard you try, your mind keeps dredging up re-writes and projections. When this takes root, and you can't seem to shake it, it helps to treat your mind like a third party and say, "Aha, I see what you're doing!" Learning to notice your thoughts as an outside observer lessens the monopoly they have on your mind. Just a little distance can create a shift so you can actually relax.

Is There a Lazy Way to Heaven?

THE LAZY WOMAN'S SPIRITUAL JOURNEY

Question

As If

Yin/Yang

Control

Death

Loss

God

Prayer

Contentment

Gratitude

Grace

INTRODUCTION

In Japan – and increasingly now in the United States – people use the beautiful art of the tea ceremony as a meditation practice. By focusing on each of the steps – from arranging the room, to making and serving the tea – each part of the preparation is a meditation. There is freedom found in the detailed focus, love in the perfection of each step, and grace in every movement. It is an honor to be a part of such a ceremony, and a blessing to be able to participate in such a sacred act.

Even though it doesn't often feel like it, life is a sacred act, a gift that we are given for a short amount of time. The more that we can appreciate each and every step along the road between our birth and death, honoring the process - the before, the after, the during - the more we will find peace in our lives.

Take this one step at a time. You can focus for quite a while on the serving of the tea with love and grace until it shifts something inside you. In the same way, you can focus on parenting your children with gratitude and sweetness, and see where that meditation leads you. You don't need to do it all at once, but if you can start to honor each moment – not judging if it is "positive" or "negative" – your heart and mind will open. The parts of your life, like the tea ceremony, will slowly begin to link together and become one fluid, dance-like process.

QUESTION

> *Be patient toward all that is unresolved in your heart and try to love the questions themselves.*

– Rainer Maria Rilke

Your "inner conversation," what's going on inside your head, creates your experience of life. Our minds are constantly assessing what we experience: work, school, a party, a meeting, or a conversation. We deem them "great," "terrible," "boring," "a waste of time," etc. Mixed in with this constant judgment are the questions.

The questions you ask determine the depth of your inner conversation. Are you asking: How do I make more money? Why don't I ever "get" the man I want? How come I didn't win the lottery? Why did I get this disease? What did I do to deserve this? These are whining, dead-end questions. There's nothing to be gained from pondering them.

> *Always the beautiful answer.
> Who asks a more beautiful question.*

– e.e. cummings

There are questions without answers that can lead to a richer life. A Zen riddle, called a *koan* in Japanese, is a question without an answer. These are asked of a student to force her, through contemplation, to a greater awareness. These are questions to engage with, not to be answered by thought or discussion. The questions worth pondering have no answers. Just allow them to float in and out of your consciousness. This creates a lazy kind of dream state that allows you to step back from your judgments and fears: Who am I? What is the meaning of life? Why am I alive in this place and time? What's the lesson in this?

The search, the questions, the process is everything. Surrendering to the mystery of life instead of having to find answers brings you serenity. The living, day by day, moment by moment, question by question, choice by choice is life.

Notice in your own inner conversation what questions you are asking. Are you attached to getting certain answers? Do you hang on to your opinions or need to have all the answers? *Make peace with the questions and the answers will appear as your life unfolds.*

As If

Bridget's father always played a game with her when she complained about not being able to find something. He would say, "If you knew where it was, where would it be?" The point of the technique, like the point of the "As If" technique, is that if you get out of your head, then you have a chance to get unstuck and inspired. You can breathe a little life into something, jostle it loose with a fresh perspective.

We all played pretend when we were kids. The "As If" technique is just one big game of pretend that will actually offers practical results. When you feel like you are a bad mom, act as if you think you are a great mom.

Act as if you are sweet and considerate if people say you are bitchy or mean. If you feel unattractive, try acting as if you know you are beautiful. Act as if you are *not* frustrated with the problem at hand. If you are struggling with depression, act as if you are happy.

> " *Act as if you were already happy and that will tend to make you happy.* "
>
> – Dale Carnegie

This is by no means a solution to what can be a very serious problem, but it can help alleviate some of the pain. Even if we can fool ourselves for a little while, it can break through the negativity that is blocking our energy and lead us to action.

YIN/YANG

On an episode of "Oprah," author Isabel Allende spoke about the very American phenomenon that we feel we have a "right" to be happy. She laughed that we even have in our Constitution the "right to the pursuit of happiness." Her laughter came from her own acceptance that life is about both happiness and sadness, the dark and the light.

Ms. Allende spoke eloquently of the year she spent caring for her daughter who was in a coma, and who ultimately died. This was followed soon after – in the same room – by another daughter giving birth to a granddaughter. The moment of birth in contrast to the moment of her daughter's death – the opposites – gave her a unique and profound revelation.

> "Some of you say 'Joy is greater than sorrow'
> and others say 'Nay, sorrow is the greater'
> But I say unto you, they are inseparable.
> Together they come, and when one sits,
> alone with you at your board,
> remember that the other is asleep upon your bed."

– *On Joy and Sorrow* by Kahlil Gibran

Embracing these opposites will actually bring ease to your life. Chinese philosophy says the world is made up of Yin and Yang, and acknowledges the beauty of the two opposing elements, which dovetail to create all that exists. We can look at the opposites in our daily lives as necessary parts that make the whole what it is, including pain and pleasure, bitter and sweet, happy and sad. This isn't always easy, but the contemplation of the dual nature of life offers some relief.

We want to cut out what we perceive as negative and edit our lives and family members' lives to include only the "positive." Even knowing that growth most often comes out of pain or difficulty, we still want to make everything "nice." But we would lose so much if we deprive ourselves of the Yin or the Yang. Accept the opposites - they can take you to powerful places.

CONTROL

Control is a sneaky animal. There are several species. There's the telling-people-what-to-do kind of control that is obvious. But the most insidious kind of control is one that we don't always admit we are exerting, when we subtly massage a situation in our favor. We all do it. If by chance you think you don't, you might want to ask someone you work or live with to help enlighten you.

It's helpful to become aware of the ways you are controlling. Where do you draw lines in the sand about how others should behave, feel, act, react? What a time-consuming job!

If you admit to yourself when you are controlling, you might just realize that it takes too much darned effort and choose to let go. Having kids is a blessing in this arena, because they nail you when your controlling nature gets out of hand. It's OK to deny it to save face, as long as you admit it to yourself, and attempt to change. Whatever brings it to your attention, try to greet it with a laugh, because control's greatest enemy is humor.

> " *We are deeply asleep at the switch when we fancy we control any switches at all.* "
>
> – Annie Dillard

The irony about control, though, is that on the deepest level we have none. If you can understand this, then how you experience life completely changes. Instead of thinking, "If I do this, then I can make that happen," you will do things without predicting or expecting a certain outcome. What you do won't necessarily change, but the burden will be lighter. It's an exhausting job to be pulling all those strings. Feel free to let go!

If you are having a tough time with this, it might be helpful to use the mantra from the Lazy Woman's Commandment #4: "I rest in the hands of God." Handing control over to God is such a relief.

DEATH

Death is a subject most of us avoid talking about and even try to avoid thinking about. We are conditioned to live in a state of denial. It's something that happens to *other* people and other people's friends and family. It isn't until something breaks this barrier that thoughts of death sneak into our world. Thinking about death, becoming obsessed with thoughts of death, is terrifying. It is part of the human condition to banish the reality of death to a hidden part of the forest.

Judie: *I was 26 years old, had just given birth to my third daughter, and my father-in-law was in intensive care, not expected to live. I was taking a bath when it started. My mind went from thinking about whether my father-in-law would live, to my own mortality, to the mortality of my children. My heart began to race, I was short of breath – I thought I was having a heart attack. When I called my doctor, he prescribed a tranquilizer over the telephone (mind you, it was 1970), and I spent the next couple of years trying to stop taking tranquilizers and re-gain my emotional stability. I tried to keep the "death thing" out of my consciousness so I could be a happy person – a good wife and mother. Later I recognized this not only as post-partum depression, but as the opening of the metaphysical closet that had been locked since my childhood: the knowledge that everyone I knew and loved would someday die, even me.*

Now, some may think that the Lazy Woman's Way would be to keep the "death thing" locked in the closet. However, consciously bringing it out into the light of day is the best way to disarm death and let it lead us to a fuller appreciation of life. Awareness of mortality can heighten our ability to experience the present moment.

> *Death sits with his key in my lock. Not one day is taken for granted.*

– Anne Sexton

Judie: *When I was thirty-six my father died in his sleep while my husband and I were traveling in Paris with my parents. We were able to stay alone in the hotel room with my father's body the whole day. I lay sobbing on the bed with my head on my father's chest. I talked to him, telling him how much I loved him, crying to my mother about how I didn't get to tell him so before he died. After many hours my mind was empty. I had gone from pure grief, to selfish concern about how my life would change, and how my first trip to Europe was over. I was empty and spent. Then my dad began speaking to me. His message sounded throughout my whole body. He said, "Don't worry. I'm still here. I'll always be with you. Everything is going to be all right." I asked my husband and my mother if they had heard him. How could they not have? When they said no, I told them what had happened. I then had two totally conflicting experiences happening within me. I was experiencing the tragic loss of my father and an exhilarating connection with him. I was truly blissed out. We flew home, made arrangements, buried my father, settled my mother, and returned to Europe. Every moment of my life was blessed. Through the years I have had moments where the sense of life's perfection embraces me, but it was the weeks following my dad's death that taught me how magical all of life is.*

" *Death, and its ever present possibility makes love, passionate love, more possible. I wonder if we could love passionately, if ecstasy would be possible at all, if we knew we'd never die.* "

– Abraham Maslow, from a letter written while recuperating from a heart attack

LOSS

Loss is part of the ebb and flow of life, the beginnings and the endings. It comes in many shapes, sizes, and depths: the end of a relationship or career, a move, lengthy illness, unmet expectations, or an empty nest. Each of the losses we experience prepare us for life's ultimate losses: losing loved ones and, of course, our own death.

Bridget: *I was recently mourning the loss of two cats that I had lost within weeks of each other. The first loss was so great…and then the second. I was complaining to a friend, asking, 'Why does God make our pets' lives so much shorter than ours?' She said she thought it was God's way of helping us practice for the greater losses in life. I thought to myself, 'Isn't this loss big enough?' But I realized that what I gained from my pets' short lives far outweighed the pain of the loss, and that my heart was richer for having had them all for at least a time.*

By consciously grieving, we take advantage of the opportunities that God gives us to be prepared in a way that will help us to actually live more fully.

S'MORNING, S'AFTERNOON, S'EVENING

Bridget's friend, Adelaide, made a most powerful and poignant observation in dealing with the death of her very loved husband of 63 years, Alec.

In the days and weeks following Alec's death, Adelaide realized that "taking it one day at a time" was far too big a hurdle to handle. She recalled the diary she kept when she was 9 years old, in which she divided each day into three sections: S'Morning, S'Afternoon and S'Evening – with entries for each part of the day. Adelaide decided to break up her days just as she did back then. She could deal with getting through the tough days with this small adjustment. This way if one part of her day ended up being not-so-wonderful, she would have a chance to balance it out with something positive, making the whole day into something that wasn't completely obscured by the loss of her love.

DEALING WITH LOSS CONSCIOUSLY

ACKNOWLEDGE AND EXPRESS THE FEELINGS: Fear, pain, anger, despair. There is no formula for the intensity or duration, no right or wrong feelings. The see-saw of emotions is part of the process.

DON'T GET STUCK: Feelings of "why me?," "why this?" are natural. But getting stuck in self-pity doesn't let you move through the pain back into life, stronger and more aware of how precious every moment is.

ASK FOR HELP: This is not the time to grin and bear it. Accept the support of family, friends, counselors or support groups.

LET YOURSELF LAUGH: Laughter does not diminish the severity of your loss. You can honor the dead with laughter as well as tears.

CHOOSE TO GO ON WITH YOUR LIFE: The best gift you can give to the memory of a lost loved one is to celebrate their life *and* yours.

GOD

"We must offer ourselves to God like a clean, smooth canvas and not worry ourselves about what God may choose to paint on it, but at each moment feel only the stroke of his brush."

– Jean-Pierre de Caussade

Call God a "Higher Power," "God Almighty," or any of the 1001 man-made names. It doesn't matter: God transcends all images. Whether you have a formal religious practice or have your own private relationship with God, the Lazy Woman reminds herself regularly that ultimately, there is no will but God's.

Often our minds can't accept the concept of not having ultimate control. We decide whether it's a problem that God needs to take care of, or one that we should handle. Sometimes, we offer to give God a break and decide that he doesn't need to get involved. Aren't we thoughtful? Some of us look at God as a magic genie who can only be called upon so many times during a lifetime, and we don't want to waste our turns asking for help, unless it's a "biggie."

Accepting the concept that God has the ultimate control does not mean that you become inactive. There is a wonderful parable about a man whose village was being flooded. The man stood on his porch as the waters began to rise. Someone drove by and offered him the last ride out of town. The man refused, proclaiming that he would survive. As the waters rose, he moved to his second floor window. Someone came by in a canoe offering to rescue him. The man again refused, saying he would be fine. Later, as he sat on his roof, a helicopter came by and pleaded with him, offering the one last escape. Again, he refused. The man perished and when he met God in heaven, he said, "I had faith that you would save me." God responded, "I sent a car, a boat, and a helicopter, what more could I do?"

You can offer the burden of finding a solution to God, but you still need to participate in moving through a situation. Your job is the "doing," praying, and practice of faith without the burden of figuring out how it is all going to be resolved.

Bridget: *I recently heard of the concept of "The God Box." You take a box and every time you have something you need God to help you with, you write it down and put it in the box. It's like God's "In-Box." It's a good way to consciously invite God to help you.*

CONTENTMENT

Feeling satisfied, feeling fulfilled, feeling like you're actually present in your own life – sometimes these feelings are few and far between. Days go by and you can't remember one truly satisfying moment, one time that you felt content. Luckily, the Lazy Woman has many positive, small, no-cost choices for creating contentment.

Bridget: *At a recent luncheon with four women, one of my friends asked us to give her our secret to contentment. The first woman excitedly chimed in that finding a good man to take care of her was her secret. The second woman, much younger than the rest of us, moaned and then sat baffled in silence by such a weighty question. I thought about the times I was happy, and realized it was usually a choice. I said I thought it was about choosing to appreciate what I did have and vigilantly avoiding focusing on the negative.*

It's so easy to focus on the negative. The media feeds on our sense of discontent. They need us to buy that which will make us happy.

> ❝*The happy man is the man who curbs his wants.*❞

– Henry David Thoreau

The trick is to remember that contentment really is yours for the having, it's right there inside you. We've all heard that you can't buy happiness, that you can't find it outside yourself, and yet we are still pulled outward. It feels like our natural instinct is to look outside ourselves.

Yet our most natural state is happy. Babies rest in the most simple and wondrous contentment; their anger or discomfort is fleeting. Nothing outside ourselves can take that away from us unless we give it the attention and power to do so.

Don't allow it! And, if you can't sway your mind from the pendulum of negativity, try to act "as if" you were content. (See As If.) Pretend you are happy, and enjoy more energy and vigor to greet the rest of your lazy life!

GRACE

Amazing grace how sweet the sound
That saved a wretch like me
I once was lost but now I'm found
Was blind but now I see.

– Traditional Hymn

Some people feel they have to work at having or keeping their faith. They struggle daily with defining or connecting to their faith. Yet, just on the other side of this struggle lies an oasis, where the blind can see. It is the land of grace. You don't have to struggle to get to it; it simply is. You can dip into it any time. It's a matter of being open to it.

Sometimes, it's easier said than done, but contemplating the concept of grace is a wonderful start. Practice accepting grace into your heart, and you will begin to appreciate the things you were perhaps "blind to" before.

ACCEPTING GRACE: A MEDITATION

Find a place that is **comfortable** and **quiet**. It can be anywhere…just so long as you can remain undisturbed for a few minutes. You can light a candle if you wish, or incense, if either of these help you create a sacred space for yourself. You can also do this in bed, before you rise or before you fall asleep at night.

Close your eyes, take a few deep breaths, paying attention to each breath as it goes in and out. Try to imagine the **breath** moving all the way from the top of your head down to the bottom of your feet.

Imagine being showered with a beautiful pink light. Allow the light to fall sweetly on you. Watch as the light rays transform into delicate pink rose petals gently showering down upon you from above, falling softly around you. Imagine the petals brushing your face, shoulders, landing on your head, knees, feet. You may even start to smell their beautiful aroma. This soft shower can last as long as you want to. Perhaps it will stop and then begin again. Enjoy it as you create it. **Envision** this as the **shower of grace**, an endless supply of love from above.

Before you rise from your journey, take a moment to **express your gratitude** for the grace that is in your life, the grace that we sometimes have trouble seeing or feeling. Say thank you for whatever you can…from the mundane to the grand. Don't stress yourself thinking of what you "should" be grateful for, just allow things to come to mind, even if the list is short…

After you have done this meditation, it may be easier to notice the ways that **grace** reveals itself in your life.

ACCEPTING GRACE ON THE RUN

Even in the midst of a busy day, you can open your heart to experience the gift of grace. If you're stuck in traffic, waiting in the carpool or checkout line...take a moment to shift your attention from the frustration of wasted time to the grace that is resting inside you at every moment of the day. You may not immediately change your thinking or feeling, but even a brief shift of focus can open your heart to the grace of God within you.

GRATITUDE

Remember when you were a child and you wanted something you couldn't have, and your mom would tell you to appreciate what you did have, to "count your blessings?" Maybe you didn't want to eat the salmon patties she made for dinner, and she would remind you about all the starving people in the world. Well, mom was right. We aren't suggesting you need to eat foods you hate, but it's always a good idea to count your blessings.

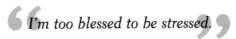
I'm too blessed to be stressed.

– Deion Sanders

Many of us remember to give thanks on Thanksgiving, or on a good day when it's easy to be grateful. But it's much harder when life is not matching your pictures. Ironically, if your spirits need lifting, gratitude can come to the rescue.

Thank You God
"The List"

Whether you're having a particularly bad day or a wonderful day, **lift your spirit** by giving thanks for the simple gifts of daily life.

There are a lot of basics that we tend to take for granted. Or we compare ourselves with others, negating what we do have. Focusing on the things you do have will slowly bring you to a more grateful attitude. Count your blessings (whether it's when you go to bed, when you wake up, or whenever you think about it). Acknowledge the smallest things: your sight, your ability to breathe and move, etc. Enjoying what you have is much more satisfying than worrying about what you don't have.

PRAYER

Prayer is a great assistance to a lazy life, and it comes in many forms. We are not talking about specific prayers of any particular religion. How you choose to silently acknowledge God, or a "higher power," is unimportant. The benefits are all the same: you release the burden to be right, to have all the answers, to God.

There will always be concerns or difficulties, but when you keep turning the solution over to God, the work on your part is much easier. Whether you repeat a Lazy Woman's Commandment, count your blessings, renew your faith, accept grace, let go of control, or choose forgiveness, you are praying. Some say the greatest prayer is simply "Thank You." Whatever your definition may be – it's your prayer and it's perfect!

Some people may not know what prayer is until they find themselves, or a loved one in a dire situation. A friend of ours, recently called from her mother's hospital room, saying she had never prayed her entire 42 years, and that she hoped she was doing it "right." Little did she know that the love that she was bestowing upon her mother *was* a prayer, the attention she gave to the nurses and doctors ensuring her mother's care was a prayer, the way that she spoke to her mother, and for her mother (who could not speak), was a prayer. With great love and respect, she honored her mother and the power that was greater than both of them. Her heart was "prayerful."

> *More things are wrought by prayer*
> *Than this world dreams of.*

– Lord Alfred Tennyson

Sometimes, we find that we have been praying all along, but that we never recognized it. We're not talking about the "Please God, let me win the lottery" kind of praying. The words are far less important than the intention. If the intention is prayerful, how can it not have a wonderful benefit – at least on your own heart, if not on others. This is about turning to God (or whatever your definition of a higher power might be – from science to Shiva) with an open heart and mind.

THE LAZIEST PRAYERS OF ALL

When you honor someone or something with all your heart, you are honoring their true essence, honoring love, honoring that they are connected to a higher power as well. You undoubtedly have prayers you have been uttering for years. But, if you need some simple phrases to repeat in a prayerful manner (either silently or aloud), try "Thank You," "I Love You," or "Bless You."

Prayer is a very lazy way to change your mood or lift a self-involved moment. The quickest way to shift your perspective is to say The Serenity Prayer, and turn it all over to God.

> "God grant me the serenity
> to accept the things I cannot change,
> the courage to change the things I can,
> and the wisdom to know the difference."

A ROAD WORTH TRAVELING

Now that you have some idea of what we mean by the Lazy Woman's Way, we caution you to avoid using this as another measuring stick for success as a woman. You don't want to replace the "has it all, does it all" picture with the "lazier than thou" ideal.

Life will continue to serve up challenges. Everyday brings a new batch of "problems" to be solved – cranky kids, unreasonable demands at work or just more to get done than you have time for. Seeing these moments as opportunities to practice your lazy skills, can make all the difference. Whenever you try to change an old pattern, there will be times when you won't feel like it or you'll want to give up. (Trust us, we both have our very un-lazy moments.)

Instead of judging, comparing yourself with "the perfect people," or listening to internal and external negative voices, remember that falling off, shifting within the plan, is all part of the process. There is nothing to be gained from self-flagellation or regret. Pull out the Lazy Woman's Seven Commandments or flip through the book to jump-start an attitude shift. Sometimes just noticing that you're getting thrown off balance can be enough to get you back on track.

The Lazy Woman's Way is something you create or recreate moment by moment. The more you flex your lazy muscles, the easier it will be. Practice letting go – of judgment, having to be right, and needing everything to be perfect. In the beginning you may feel it's impossible, or at the very least, frightening. As they say in the Twelve-Step Programs, "Keep coming back." It's in the coming back that you walk the Lazy Woman's path. Falling off is just part of the journey.

Once you understand that there is no failure in the Lazy Woman's Way, it removes the pressure, the weight of having to *do* or *be* anything.

Remember, keep coming back!

The Lazy Woman's Seven Commandments are tools to help you *live* the Lazy Woman's philosophy, to help you cultivate that inner lazy attitude.

Put copies in your pocket or purse, on your fridge, or over your desk. Use them when something is making you cranky, weighing you down, or pushing your buttons. Even if you have no idea what's bothering you, don't get stuck trying to figure it out, go straight to letting go, which is what these Commandments are all about. Let them move you to a more relaxed state. Often solutions appear seemingly out of nowhere when your mind is calm. Although circumstances may remain the same, you will be more at ease, which always leads to better choices.

THE COMMANDMENTS

1. THIS TOO SHALL PASS.

Whatever worries you today will be ancient history in the future. It can be big issues – like illness, relationship problems or financial difficulties, or small annoyances – like social disappointments, too much to do or derailed plans. Whatever it is that's bothering you, it's only made more difficult by dwelling on it. Living with the awareness that "This too shall pass" also helps prepare you for Commandment #2!

Affirmations: "This too shall pass"...or... "I won't always feel this way"...

2. EXPERIENCE THE MOMENT YOU ARE LIVING WHILE YOU ARE LIVING IT.

This moment is your life. True happiness can only be experienced in this moment. When things are not going according to your plans, remember to turn away from your inner debates and tune in to the people and activities around you right now. And, on the flip side, remember to enjoy the good times, too!

Say: "This moment is my life"…or… "Let me savor every moment."

3. TAKE PLEASURE IN WHAT YOU HAVE.

Taking a moment to give thanks for what you have is always grounding. Notice the warmth of the morning sun on your face or savor the taste of the hot tea. Give thanks for the good things large and small: from sweet fresh water to gas for the car, your eyesight, or the sound of the birds outside.

Repeat: "I appreciate"…or …"I give thanks for…"

4. YOU ARE RESTING IN THE HANDS OF GOD (THE UNIVERSE).

There is nothing to control. Of course, you have to go about the business of your life. But, it is the belief that you actually have to control the outcome that creates a burden. Letting go of that control allows you to move through the situations in your life with greater ease.

Mantra: "I rest in the hands of God"…or… "There is nothing I need to control …"

5. YOU CAN EITHER BE RIGHT OR BE HAPPY.

When your mind is stuck in judgment, you are not happy. If you need to be right, and get upset when others disagree with you, you are only hurting yourself. There are as many different viewpoints as there are people. You can have your opinion; just don't let them block you from accepting others.

Mantra: "I choose to be happy"...or "I don't need to be right."

6. PUT YOUR ATTENTION OUTSIDE OF YOURSELF.

If you are in a deep pit, it is often difficult to redirect your mind. It may take several steps: a favorite video, audiotape, gardening, playing with your pet or reaching out to someone else. Do something that draws your attention to living in the moment – get outside of your thoughts. When you slip back into mind chatter just notice it and once again look outward.

Mantra: "I wake up to the life around me..."

7. YOU ARE A SEPARATE PERSON. YOU ARE NOT YOUR (MOTHER, HUSBAND, BOSS, LOVER...).

When you take on someone else's pain, frustration and problems, or get hooked into their criticism of you, there is no peace. No matter how much you love someone, their life is not yours and their opinions do not rule you. You can't take care of everyone, or please everyone. Lazy Women think living one life is just about enough.

Mantra: "I can only live my life."...or... "I allow you to live your life."

"I make no secret of the fact that I would rather lie on the sofa than sweep beneath it. But you have to be efficient if you're going to be lazy."

– Shirley Conran

Shortcuts and timesavers add up to more Hammock Time for the Lazy Women. When you make things easier in little ways, it slows down the hurried pace of life. Becoming aware of who and what deserves your effort, and eliminating the "drainers," frees you for the people and activities that enrich the quality of each day.

THE PRACTICAL TIPS

1. USE WHAT YOU HAVE.
Often you can make something work that you already have. It may be that two cans of leftover paint mixed together make the perfect color. Improvising in the kitchen can inspire some new recipes or at least save you a trip to the market.

2. KEEP IT AT HAND AND IN SIGHT.
Save time and energy by keeping duplicates of oft-used items in several places and within view (toothbrushes and toothpaste for the kids in all the bathrooms; scissors and tape in the drawer with the wrapping paper as well as in the kitchen and your desk; kitchen tools in a crock on your counter instead of in a drawer; a portable basket on your desk with scissors, tape, pencils, pens, stapler, Post-Its and Sharpies). It's not lazy to run around looking for the only roll of Scotch tape!

3. DO LESS, BE MORE.

When you are feeling overwhelmed by a situation, reduce your options. Simplify the plan. Whether it's an interior design issue, picking out an outfit, getting together a kid's party, or dinner for your boss – narrow the field of choices. Find a unifying element (color, theme) and run with it. Don't waste time worrying, and you'll enjoy the process more.

4. GET THE MOST BANG FOR YOUR BUCK.

Get maximum impact for minimum output. Find plants for your garden that take the least work and give you the most beautiful display. Choose the easiest recipe with the most spectacular results. Drink plenty of water to feel good, look good and improve your long term health. Make choices that have multiple benefits.

5. WILL IT MAKE MY LIFE EASIER?

Whether it's a piece of equipment or a piece of advice, ask yourself if it will make life more convenient or just complicate things. What's the trade-off for the convenience (or speed) factor? What's the maintenance? Can I run it or will it run me? Does this suit my style? Just because an "expert" recommends it doesn't mean it's for you.

6. TRIM THE HIGH MAINTENANCE HEDGE.

Choose where you want to put your energy. If a certain hairdo, car, wardrobe, garden, or entertaining style is worth the effort it takes, then keep it. But take a look at what things – or people – are high maintenance. You gotta love the high maintenance stuff to make it worthwhile.

7. PICK UP TIME WHERE YOU CAN.

Spend some extra time now to save time in the future. Get yourself off junk mail and telemarket lists, buy in bulk (toilet paper, detergent, etc.), or set up back-to-back doctor/dentist appointments for family members. Steal an hour here and there by giving up TV for one night, not returning phone calls, or ordering in food.

8. AVOID THE DRAINERS, EMBRACE THE ENERGIZERS.

People and activities can either give you energy or leave you feeling wiped out. The Drainers take your time and energy. The Energizers add quality and quantity to your days. Pay attention to who or what takes from your life or adds to it.

9. GIVE YOURSELF A BREAK.

Think of all the things that you don't have to do, that are self-imposed priorities. Give yourself permission to be less than perfect. Take shortcuts or drop something from your "To Do" list, and don't feel guilty about it.

10. HAVE LAZY GOALS.

Focus on something that you've wanted to do, but never got around to doing. Let this be the month or year that your fantasy rose garden gets to be a priority. But when it's no longer satisfying, give yourself permission to move on. Lazy goals should feed the soul.

THANK YOU

We received tremendous support while creating this book.

Thank God for Frances Fusco (aka, "the Comma Queen"). While working on the final edits of the book, we could both be heard uttering, "Fran wouldn't let us do that…" She kept with the lazy spirit, while making us better writers. Jeff Goldman, of Santa Monica Press, pointed us in the right direction and toward our Kissingeresque book designer, Susan Landesmann. She helped us realize our vision with patience and grace.

We thank the many women who have exclaimed, "I have to own that book!" and those who have come to our Lazy Woman Workshops. We are grateful to Kathy Kelly Gallegos and Bridget's dad, Max, for reading early drafts. Generous authors, Terry Lynn Taylor, Carol Adrienne, Kathy Eldon and Manuela Dunn urged us to keep writing. Literary agent/editor, Loretta Barrett moved us to start our Lazy Woman Workshops. Ann Muller helped us develop our Lazy Woman image. Thanks to ALL of our friends for their constant encouragement.

Special thanks to Allison Burnett for helping us proofread something that is far less than a literary masterpiece. We know how painful that was for him. Also to Annaly Benett for her last minute visual tweaking and Roberta Grady for her final read.

Among our many teachers, we acknowledge the late Deanna Eck for her insight and healing.

ACKNOWLEDGMENTS

Judie: Sister Mary Margretine, B.V.M. for urging me to keep asking questions, Father J. Sweeters, S.J. for encouraging my honesty, Dr. Michael Valente for the Course in Mastery and my greatest teachers – my family: J.P., Lisa, Lauren, Jilann, Max, Conor and Quinn.

Bridget: Gurumayi for showing me that frantic wasn't my natural state, Ramtha for giving me the shortest distance between two points, Diana Guyer and Sally Trim for being arbiters of exquisite taste, and Judie, for encouraging a lazy inner attitude, and helping me laugh at my oh-so-unlazy parts.

Our deep appreciation to Alec and Adelaide Hixon for Wickerworks, and to Kay Freund Kowal for Vista Pacifica. Thanks to Diana Guyer for her coffee farm on the Kona Coast – if there were a Lazy Woman Mecca, this very well might be it.

BOOKS

We encourage you to read any of these books just as you would read ours – a chapter at a time, cover to cover, or open them randomly for inspiration. If you need to, read and re-read them. There are some books that we've never read in their entirety that contain sections we return to over and over for inspiration and guidance. Even if you get just one idea that serves you, a book is worth exploring. We've annotated the list with some of our personal experiences about how these books have helped us.

PARENTING & FAMILY

Everyday Blessings: The Inner Work of Mindful Parenting by Myla Kabat-Zinn and Jon Kabat-Zinn

> Judie: *As the title implies, this book reminds us what it means to be a 'conscious' parent. I find that it reassures and inspires me every time I pick it up. When I am stressed about how to parent, this book helps me interact positively with my son, which always creates a better outcome*

Raising a Family, Raising a Son, Raising a Daughter and Raising a Teenager by Jeanne Elium & Don Elium

> The Eliums are the parents we all wished for! They are a husband and wife team (he is a marriage, family and child counselor and she is a transpersonal educator and workshop leader) with amazing insight into the psychological, emotional and spiritual stages of boys and girls, and the nurturing of a family. You won't know how you parented before you read their books.

All That She Can Be – Helping Your Daughter Maintain Her Self-Esteem by Dr. Carol J. Eagle and Carol Colman

Like a "Dr. Spock" for adolescent girls, this user-friendly guide is packed with examples, pertinent, practical information, a thorough index of topics, and a really great bibliography.

Reviving Ophelia: Saving the Selves of Adolescent Girls by Mary Pipher. Ph.D.

Mary Pipher uses case histories, literature and memories of her own adolescence to illustrate the struggle of adolescent girls to retain a sense of their real selves. The fourth chapter entitled "Developmental Issues – 'I'm not Waving, I'm Drowning'" has a detailed, illuminating description of what it's like to be a teenager growing up in today's society. Anyone who spends time with teenagers, boys as well as girls, should read this chapter regularly.

Strong Mothers, Strong Sons by Ann F. Caron, ED.D

This helpful guide illuminates the stages of male development and covers all the bases, including the scary adolescent ones, like anger, violence, drugs, sex and suicide. The author recommends the interdependence of boys and their mothers while giving mothers the insight and support they need to love and guide their sons through adolescence.

Emotional Intelligence by Daniel Goleman

Full of practical insights and applications, this book outlines the crucial role that our emotions play in intelligently directing our lives, and offers strategies for supporting the emotional growth of young people.

Raising Cain: Protecting the Emotional Life of Boys
by Dan Kindlon, Ph.D. and Michael Thompson, Ph.D.

In the media frenzy over the causes of boy-generated violence, many of the solutions are solely punitive, the so-called 'boot camp' approach. We are thankful that the authors have shed light on all the destructive emotional training that boys are usually given. They also present guidelines for allowing boys to experience, identify and express their feelings. The seven points for nurturing the emotional life of boys (pages 241-258) provide a terrific blueprint for parents, teachers and others who work with boys.

Our Last Best Shot – Guiding Our Children Through Early Adolescence by Laura Sessions Stepp

Judie: *I heard about this book in a radio interview and rushed out the same day to buy it. It was one of those days when I thought that I must have done something terribly wrong as a parent to raise a child that behaved like that. I wish I had read it before my son was eleven but it has saved my sanity many times since. My husband and I read and re-read the stories of what can go right or wrong depending on whether and how parents intervene. It helps me feel that my son is moving through the pitfalls of early adolescence successfully.*

The Heart of a Family: Searching America for New Traditions that Fulfill Us by Meg Cox

Whether you're looking for ideas to expand your holiday traditions, create rituals to calm nighttime fears, or honor a rite-of-passage or achievement, this book is full of personal stories and sound ideas to help guide and inspire the conscious act of creating a family.

Husband-Coached Childbirth by Robert Bradley, M.D.

Judie: *This book taught me how to make the delivery of my first child as painless as possible and help my body recover fully and quickly. These relaxation techniques have worked for me ever since. My dentist says I'm the only patient who has ever fallen asleep in his chair. Even if you're having a C-section or a medicated delivery, the ability to relax during the first stages of labor will make it quicker and more comfortable.*

The Womanly Art of Breastfeeding by La Leche League

This book has been around a long time and contains the answers to all your breastfeeding questions.

The New Mom's Manual by Mary Jeanne Menna

Loaded with tips from moms who share their favorite, most effective tips on their baby's first year, it's easy-to-read format and mom-tested tips offer inspiration and encouragement along with all the necessary baby care information.

Your Two-Year-Old, Your Three-Year-Old, and *Your Four-Year-Old,* etc. by Louise Bates Ames and Frances L. Ilg

This is a series of books on child-raising from the Gesell Institute of Child Development. They're invaluable as a resource for understanding your child's specific age. Just when you think you know them, they hit a whole new stage!

HOME

Rachel Ashwell's Shabby Chic by Rachel Ashwell

This is a sensual delight for the eyes imbued with the author's underlying philosophy of home as a living thing that develops and changes. It's fun and inspiring with charmingly illustrated restoration tips.

If I'd Only Listened to My Mom, I'd Know How to Do This by Jean B. MacLeod

Packed between the covers of this book are: brief household hints in an A-Z format, more extended information by topic, comprehensive coverage of cleaning products, an exhaustive list of useful addresses and phone numbers and an extremely detailed explanation of weights and measures. A veritable first-aid book for the homemaker!

Too Busy to Clean? by Patti Barrett

More "point-of-view" than pure cleaning information, this book provides a nice balance of tips and philosophy, with a light-hearted approach. Since we like to get-it-over-quick, this book fits our lazy style of housekeeping.

Clean and Green by Annie Berthold-Bond

This is a well laid-out recipe book for non-toxic cleaning, using stuff you've got in your cupboard. The alphabetical list of laundry stain removers is worth the price of the book. Save the planet and your health!

PSYCHOLOGICAL & EMOTIONAL

Love is Letting Go of Fear and *Good-bye to Guilt* by Gerald G. Jampolsky, M.D.

These books are based on *A Course in Miracles*, which is a self-directed form of 'spiritual therapy.' Even if you aren't interested in anything spiritual or therapeutic, these books offer an accessible path to a peaceful way of being.

The Purpose of Your Life by Carol Adrienne

Whether you feel you are truly on your life's path or you have no clue of what your purpose is, this book will reawaken your life's call from deep within. It transposes worry about your life's purpose into positive action.

The Road Less Traveled by M. Scott Peck, M.D.

An oldie but goodie, we particularly recommend the chapter on love, which hits the mark on the difference between romantic and real love.

Homecoming: Reclaiming and Championing Your Inner Child by John Bradshaw

Many therapists recommend this book as a starting point to become more aware of what's behind dysfunctional behavior. If you are in pain, this book may offer insight and a salve for the heart. Look at the first chapter and if it resonates with you, this book will probably be quite helpful.

Relationship Rescue: 10 Myths About Connecting With Your Partner by Phillip C. McGraw, Ph.D.

Bridget: *Phil McGraw really cuts to the quick of an issue. When I see him on "Oprah," I am always impressed by his straightforward, sobering manner. Yet, he has such compassion that I am always hopeful that I can tackle some of my heavier issues.*

Alcoholics Anonymous by Alcoholics Anonymous World Services, Inc.

This is the "big book," the basic text for Alcoholics Anonymous. It was originally published in 1939 and yet contains wisdom that has been translated into many of the other books on this list. It is definitely not just for alcoholics. You will find yourself in someone else's story, and if any kind of addiction burdens your life, this is the place to start.

INSPIRATIONAL & SPIRITUAL

What Would Buddha Do? by Franz Metcalf

Although the introduction includes a brief presentation of Buddha, you don't have to be a follower to find this book helpful and inspiring. It addresses some of life's daily dilemmas and allows this great teacher to lead the way. We love the author's humorous, direct, cut-to-the-chase application of profound wisdom.

Way of the Peaceful Warrior by Dan Millman

This is the first of Dan Millman's books, which inspire with great simplicity. Out of the story of two people meeting comes a profound philosophy of life. Though written for teenagers and adults, its insight can be shared with children in *Secret of the Peaceful Warrior*.

The Seat of the Soul and *Soul Stories* by Gary Zukav

The Seat of the Soul is a challenging, inspiring and life-changing book. If you find it daunting (un-lazy) read it over a period of time, or use our 'ask for guidance, open it randomly' method, and get a needed shift or new direction. *Soul Stories* is filled with fascinating stories that illustrate the more abstract concepts presented in the first book.

Tuesdays with Morrie by Mitch Albom

Morrie Schwartz's wisdom – in living and dying – was a great gift to his student, Mitch Albom, who shares that treasure with readers. If you're having trouble in the 'gratitude' arena, read this book.

The Measure of Our Days – New Beginnings at Life's End by Jerome Groopman, M.D.

This is a hard book to read (for instance, Bridget wouldn't be able to read through her tears), but it is amazing and inspiring. You will be awed by the people that Dr. Groopman chronicles, and by his ability to open himself up again and again to caring for people who are suffering, facing death and yet are so much more fully alive than most of us.

A Course in Miracles – Text, Workbook for Students, Manual for Teachers by Foundation for Inner Peace

We have both had great experiences with this course, but we have also both done it in our own way. We took the introduction seriously when it told us not to try to understand the text. This can be a problem for some people. So, if the thought of not understanding something makes you crazy, you should either avoid this book like the plague, or run out and get it now.

Meditation for Busy People by Dawn Groves

Even if it's only a momentary timeout to bring your mind back into the present moment, meditation is a lifesaver. No matter how far you choose to take it, this book is a good place to start.

The Complete Tales & Poems of Winnie-the-Pooh by A.A. Milne

A lazy way to jostle yourself out of a bad mood.

Bridget: *I have my Winnie-the-Pooh book next to my bed because when I can't muster up a smile, this is my cure. People may think these stories are written just for kids, but there is sophisticated humor throughout. Just picturing Piglet trying to kidnap Roo pulls me out of a bad mood! If it's not Pooh, find a book that lifts your spirits and have it near.*

MARRIAGE/RELATIONSHIPS

Passionate Marriage: Love, Sex, Intimacy in Emotionally Committed Relationships by David Schnarch

> Bridget: *You don't have to be married or even in a romantic relationship to appreciate the insights in this book. It will enhance every relationship you have by helping you become more authentic, and therefore making your relationships far more intimate and fulfilling. Plus, sprinkled throughout are great little sex stories to keep you awake.*

The New Couple – Why the Old Rules Don't Work and What Does by Maurice Taylor and Seana McGee

> For couples of all kinds, this book is the "magic bullet." Filled with simple checklists, basic principles and powerful examples, it's a must-read (and re-read) book.

HEALTH

Well Being for Women by Stella Weller

> A great resource for overall health and well being, this book uses drawings, photos, lists, charts, helpful hints and exercises to support the concise coverage of this huge topic in only 125 pages.

How to Save Your Own Life by Marie Savard, M.D. with Sondra Forsyth

> This is the book to help you be the keeper of your own health. If you are well, it's a matter of keeping up with

basic health checks. If you are dealing with a chronic condition or health crisis it will serve as a road map for managing your care.

150 Most Asked Questions About Menopause
by Ruth S. Jacobowitz

Fact-filled and easy to access, this small book has much to offer about this passage of life. One caveat: the jury is still out on HRT, so continue to consult other sources for up-to-the-minute information.

You're Not Old Until You're Ninety: Best to Be Prepared, However by Rebecca Latimer

This woman is inspiring no matter how old you are, but for anyone past "middle age" she is the role model you've been waiting for. Her zest for living life to the fullest permeates each page. As she says, "The way I see it, the first rule is to be open to new ideas, to be non-judgmental... an open mind will take you further than you think."

Natural Health, Natural Medicine: A Comprehensive Manual for Wellness and Self-Care by Andrew Weil, M.D.

This is the bible of preventative medicine. From arnica to yoga, Dr. Weil has organized a tremendous amount of information in an easy-to-read, practical format.

MONEY

The Nine Steps to Financial Freedom by Suze Orman

If you have "money issues" or face a financial crisis and need an immediate Rx, this book offers sound and simple advise and contains a comprehensive index so you can zero in on your problem area. Suze Orman also has a weekly radio show which is syndicated in most major markets.

TAPES, CDS AND OTHER STUFF

Many of these tapes come in book form, of course, but with reading time being very limited, tapes are a wonderful way to do 'double time.' You can be commuting, cooking or cleaning out drawers, *and* get inspiration or information.

The Energy of Money – A Spiritual Guide to Financial and Personal Fulfillment by Maria Nemeth, Ph.D.

Bridget: *If you have issues around money, this is a relatively painless way of getting through them. Ms. Nemeth has a great conversational and compassionate way about her, which makes facing these hard issues so much easier.*

There is a Spiritual Solution to Every Problem by Dr. Wayne W. Dyer

Starting with a statement from *A Course in Miracles*, "you don't have any problems; you only think you do," Dr. Dyer presents the case for how the mind controls both physical and emotional well-being. This is an entertaining and enlightening set of tapes which can give you the tools to 'change your mind.'

Why People Don't Heal and *Spiritual Power, Spiritual Practice* from The Caroline Myss Audio Collection

We use these tapes as mini-retreats. On a long commute, they can calm and inform you as you drive. Even if you've read her books, the tapes refresh and reinforce the information – all the better to help you apply it.

The Heart of Parenting – Raising an Emotionally Intelligent Child by John Gottman, Ph.D. with Joan De Claire

Judie: *The first time I listened to this tape, I happened to be on my way to pick up my son at school. When I saw his scowling face as he threw his backpack into the car, I flashed on a technique I had just heard on the tape. I consciously applied the technique and within a few minutes we were sharing an after school snack and a light moment. I still don't always "get it right" but the insights I've gotten from John Gottman are teaching me how to help my son better understand and express his emotions.*

Ageless Body, Timeless Mind – The Quantum Alternative to Growing Old by Deepak Chopra

Just listening to these tapes takes wear and tear off your body.

Rain Dance, Mountain Light, Traveler and Miracles by Rob Whitesides-Woo.

We love the music of Rob Whitesides-Woo for relaxing and meditating. Rich with magical sounds, his music

will lead you to the stillness of your heart. Contact
Serenity Productions at (800) 869-1684 to order.

NECESSARY LUXURIES FOR A LAZY LIFE

Pawley's Island Hammocks – The official lazy place to
buy the best hammock in the world is The Hammock
Shop! They have an easy-to-navigate website at
www.hammockshop.com, and very helpful sales people at
(800) 332-3490.

Trader Joe's – The Lazy Woman's dream when it comes
to daily meals for your family, or even dinner parties for
discerning palates. If you don't have a Trader Joe's in
your city yet, you may have one very soon because they
are a hit wherever they land, and are expanding fairly rapidly. They have fresh, high quality, easy-to-use foods for
the pantry, refrigerator and freezer. You can't help but
create deliciousness when you shop there.

CATALOGUES/ONLINE

You don't even have to get out of your pajamas to shop!
Leafing through your favorite catalogues or perusing a
website, even when you don't buy, can help satisfy a shopping craving. We find these catalogues and websites particularly comforting.

Renaissance Books & Tapes (www.renaissancebks.com or www.audiosource.com)

This is a great source for all kinds of books and tapes with a strong collection in the spiritual, motivational arena (i.e. from Robert Ludlum to Gary Zukav).

Chinaberry Catalog (www.Chinaberry.com or 1-800-776-2242)

This catalog is dedicated to offering books and items to support families in raising their children with love, honesty, and joy. There are personal reviews of each book. We find that just browsing through the catalog inspires us.

A Common Reader (www.commonreader.com or 1-800-832-7323)

You can get lost in this catalogue and feel much rewarded by any time that has passed. Keep it next to your bed for a quick nightcap read.

The Company of Books (www.commonreader.com or 1-800-832-7323)

This catalogue is full of books that are great "company" for children. The descriptions and illustrations alone are a good bedtime read.

Isabella (www.IsabellaCatalog.com)

This catalog offers books, tools, and other inspirations for supporting spiritual growth and reverence for life. Their product selection is directed at women who are interested in finding their true passion, nurturing their creativity and taking care of their bodies.

Sounds True (www.soundstrue.com or 1-800-333-9185)

This catalog offers audio, video and music to nourish the inner life. Many of the selections are what would be called 'spiritual' but there are also some with very practical information on health and fitness or with home/work applications.

LAZY NOTES

LAZY NOTES

We hope you've enjoyed our book. If you want to share stories about how you've made your life lazy, please email us at www.lazywoman.com or write us c/o the publisher. For information on future Lazy Woman books and products, contact:

Elephant Eye Press
P.O. Box 50250
Pasadena, CA 91115-0250
www.elephanteyepress.com

This book may be ordered from the publisher, *but please try your local bookstore first!*